THE GREAT PARANORMAL CLASH

THE GREAT PARANORMAL CLASH

Dr. Ciarán O'Keeffe and Billy Roberts

Foreword by Jane Goldman

APEX PUBLISHING LTD

Hardback first published in 2008 by
Apex Publishing Ltd
PO Box 7086, Clacton on Sea, Essex, CO15 5WN, England
www.apexpublishing.co.uk

Copyright © 2008 by Dr. Ciarán O'Keeffe and Billy Roberts
The authors have asserted their moral rights

British Library Cataloguing-in-Publication Data
A catalogue record for this book
is available from the British Library

ISBN HARDBACK: 1-906358-14-1   978-1-906358-14-3

All rights reserved. This book is sold subject to the condition, that no part of this book is to be reproduced, in any shape or form. Or by way of trade, stored in a retrieval system or transmitted in any form or by any means, electronic, mechanical, photocopying, recording, be lent, re-sold, hired out or otherwise circulated in any form of binding or cover other than that in which it is published and without a similar condition, including this condition being imposed on the subsequent purchaser, without prior permission of the copyright holder.

Typeset in 10.5pt Gill Sans MT

Production Manager: Chris Cowlin

Cover Design: Siobhan Smith

Printed and bound in Great Britain by
Biddles Ltd., King's Lynn, Norfolk

From Billy Roberts:
I would like to dedicate this book to my wife Dolly, for her understanding and support.
I would also like to give my thanks to Ciarán O'Keeffe, for showing enough interest in my work and for sharing his thoughts and expertise with me in writing this book.

Introduction
By Ciarán O'Keeffe

Our first meetings were a little tense. In fact, the very first time we met, any outside observer might have thought it had the same tense atmosphere as a duel. We were literally "throwing down the gauntlet" before anything was said. The Parapsychologist was raising a provocative eyebrow and almost saying "prove it" whilst The Clairvoyant was saying "prove I can't". The seed of a dialogue between two different sides of the paranormal was planted.

When we originally discussed this project we had visions of it being "The Parapsychologist versus The Clairvoyant", a battle between two opposing viewpoints. After numerous extended lunches at the Neighbourhood Café when our viewpoints became concrete and our openness towards each other became cemented over a glass of wine, we realised this wasn't a battle. My sceptical view is frequently misinterpreted as cynical. Billy, likewise, has his sceptical, and even cynical, moments. The book was ultimately written by us by coming up with topics we wanted to discuss. Sometimes this resulted in a brief discussion over lunch, sometimes it merely entailed one of us giving a topic area or chapter title to the other. We would, for the most part, write our parts independently of each other. We'd then pull together a few chapters and read them, noting down questions and then returning them to the other for a response. So the format became sections where we introduced various paranormal topics and each gave our views on them, intertwined with question sections where we each interrogated the other. This continued until we realised we needed to stop somewhere. There are so many topics to cover in the paranormal that this had the potential of being an encyclopaedia rather than a book. When you take a glance at some of the topics discussed but not included or those still to cover you'll understand exactly what I mean: spirit possession, UFOS, exorcism, stigmata, reincarnation, astroarchaeology, water-divining, alien abduction, ley lines, SHC, crop circles, even lycanthropy and even chupacabra!

What you're about to read, therefore, are chapters where we have given our opinions on various paranormal topics. These opinions are based on our experience and knowledge gained over the years. Each section is headed so the reader knows who is saying what, essentially like reading two books in one. Together we present our views on all manner of paranormal phenomena, rarely seeing eye-to-eye, but never causing black eyes by aggressively punching home a point. Listen to what we each have to say, respect each viewpoint, then make up your own mind...

Ciarán O'Keeffe

Introduction
By Billy Roberts

As well as respecting his professional standing, over the years I have come to regard Ciaran O'Keeffe as a friend, and so writing this book with him has most probably been one of the most exciting projects, which I have ever undertaken. Although it might be seen as a confrontation of ideas in places, the primary motive for writing it, was to enlighten those interested in the paranormal, as to its realities and misconceptions. Even though in the book we have come to agree about many things, I am quite satisfied that we have achieved exactly what we set out to achieve.

Billy Roberts

Foreword
By Jane Goldman

Ciarán and I met in the course of making the first season of the documentary series Jane Goldman Investigates, where he accompanied us on all-night vigils, helped us to devise experiments and regularly gave us the benefit of his wealth of knowledge and expertise, both on and off camera, swiftly becoming an irreplaceable cornerstone of the programme.

Until Ciarán came along, however, the cardinal rule that my team and I had come to adopt was to do our level best to keep the makers of point and counter-point as far away from one another as possible. The contributors included mediums, psychometrists, dowsers, healers and ghost hunters, as well as ordinary individuals who had experienced extraordinary events, and many had brought with them an innate distrust of anyone from the scientific side of parapsychology, often based on previous bad experiences.

But with Ciarán, things were different. Where once there had been arguments there were now conversations. It was something of a revelation.

I came to observe, however, that true dialogue between scientist and paranormal practitioner wasn't just about tact or "people-skills", or an affable personality, but a deep understanding of the beliefs and experiences of others, a sense of curiosity, a heartfelt love of the subject and an ability to parlay all of the above into productive communication - in other words, a genuine exchange of information and ideas.

The significance of this was, to my mind, enormous. The conflicts my production team and I had observed - and frequently been caught up in! - represented in microcosm much that is problematic in the field of paranormal research. On reflection, I can't think of any other areas of scientific study where the state of relations between the scientists and their subjects was quite so poor – characterised by failures of communication at best and, at worst, downright hostility and distain from both sides. I often wondered whether it was no coincidence that progress in our understanding of anomalous human experience was so slow - as opposed to, say, our understanding of human behaviour or physical disease.

Little did I know, when I first wandered into the world of paranormal study fourteen years ago that I was, in fact, walking into a battleground. I expected conflicting theories, certainly, and varying beliefs, but where I expected to find lively debate I found something more akin to trench warfare, with pot-shots being taken by either side at anyone who stuck his head over the parapet, and a marked sense that ultimately, there was no hope of victory for either faction.

As a journalist and author of non-fiction who aspired to uphold the "Just the facts ma'am" school of neutral reporting, I found myself in no man's land. And, despite meeting a great number of intelligent and fascinating people from both sides of the battlefield, I still had a sense of wandering in isolation until I had the great good fortune to encounter Ciarán. And boy was I pleased to see him. Not just a fellow traveller through the hail of crossfire but – if you'll excuse me for stretching this already over-extended metaphor to within an inch of it's life – one who was unafraid to suggest calling a truce and having a game of intellectual football instead.

I'd also struggled with the constant pressure to categorise my approach to the subject. I had quickly learned that, in the world of paranormal enquiry, neutrality seemed not to be a tenable position, and that one could expect to be called upon with some regularity to declare one's allegiance in the most simple terms available.

The main choices, it appeared, were to be either "open-minded" or "a sceptic" – soubriquets which themselves made the issue even more confusing. For my part, I certainly considered myself open-minded (although an open-mind, like a sense of humour, is something that everyone thinks they have – even those who seem to show no evidence for it whatsoever.) But "open-minded" had, it seemed, come to mean "a person who believes in paranormal explanations for unusual phenomena". Which didn't describe me with any great accuracy. To me, theories that purported to solve life's mysteries in a way that relied on new and unproven laws of the universe were as unsatisfying as reading a fabulously intriguing whodunnit only to be told at the end that the butler did it in the locked room by magic. Suddenly the mystery is no longer mysterious, the intrigue no longer intriguing, and all we're left with is an answer that doesn't fit in with how the world works, and a whole lot more questions.

So was I a sceptic? Well, in the true sense of the word, I certainly was. But in the modern lexicon, the word is all too often used to mean "someone who does not believe in paranormal phenomena and thinks that anyone who claims otherwise is deluded or making it up". That wasn't me either. And among many smart, sincere and friendly mediums, paranormal researchers and people I'd met who'd had odd experiences of one kind or another, "sceptic" was pretty much on a par with any of the words you might reach for when addressing someone who had just rear-ended your car.

The ideal sceptic would be one who escapes from this semantic nightmare – a questioner who is both open-minded and (in the classical sense) sceptical, a shining example of one who adopts a genuine neutrality in their approach, whatever it may be. A true sceptic is not out to prove – as so many of the scientists I met seemed to be – that claims of the anomalous were there merely to be refuted, rather than understood. But neither - like so many on the non-scientific side of the fence – should they accept that some mysteries had already been solved to satisfaction.

My sheer delight at having met Ciarán, then, wasn't just about things being considerably more pleasant down the pub at the end of a day's filming (though that was certainly a nice bonus). It was about setting a template for an approach to dialogue and investigation that I still strive to emulate myself, and would unhesitatingly urge everyone, from amateurs and students to experts alike, to adopt. I've not had the pleasure of meeting Billy Roberts, but his eloquence and open-mindedness make him the ideal pairing in this journey of enquiry.

In this field what is needed is inspiration for the opposing sides to lay down their weapons and have their no-man's land match. And to my mind, this book is that game – a rousing yet civilised kick around of ideas and so much more. For it represents a powerfully significant step towards the uniting of those who experience the paranormal and those who study the world by scientific method, that can surely only lead to advancement in the further understanding of anomalous human experience.

Jane Goldman

Acknowledgements

I, Ciarán, am indebted to a number of scholars, some of whom were probably never aware of the huge impact they had made, until now: Professors James Siemen, George Spilich, Garry Clarke, Laurence Alison, Richard Wiseman and Dr. Kanthamani, (perhaps a quick thanks also to Drs Venkman, Stantz & Spengler). The scientific moulding wouldn't have been possible without the wise, and sometimes foolish, relevant words of encouragement from friends along the way. These were words that pushed me years before this book even became an idea: Tim Dyer, Tony Wright, Joe Koskuba, Nate Harned, Peter David, Pamela Reed, Kristin Stein, Lol & Emily, Andy Rose, Chris Burwood, and Emma Greening. I've met countless paranormal practitioners (charlatans, deluded and 'genuine' alike) on my journey and I'd like to thank each and every one of them in turn, there's just not the room available here to do so. You know who you are, thank you. I'd also like to thank my co-author, Billy, for his undeniable role in this Paranormal Clash double act, and also his wonderful wife, for their patience in dealing with an academic whose poor time-keeping and crazy schedule would've had lesser mortals fleeing a lot sooner. Finally my warmest thanks go to my family, my mum and dad, my brother and sister-in-law, and especially the three people who, unknowingly, in the last five years have made me truly search for the answer to Life, the Universe & Everything whilst sometimes, merely because of their presence, have left me not searching for an answer at all: Jannick, Gaëlle and Renan X.

Chapter 1:
The Parapsychologist
& The Clairvoyant

Our Backgrounds
The Parapsychologist - Ciarán O'Keeffe

When I'm in a social situation - a party, dinner in a restaurant, drinking in my local - and I mention what I do, I always get a similar reaction. "What got you into that?" "Have you ever seen anything paranormal?" "Are you a Ghost Buster?" "Let me tell you about the time…" What never happens is that I get bored of hearing these questions, of hearing about people's fascinating experiences. It's what started the whole science of Parapsychology over a century ago; it's what got me into studying the paranormal over 15 years ago.

I don't know where my interest in the area of the paranormal began. Perhaps a voracious appetite for horror novels started it all. Those secretive late nights reading classic ghost tales or gory bestsellers, planting seeds of mystery and inquiry that would last with me beyond by doctorate. Or perhaps it was the furtive glances at posters advertising the latest gore-fest, dreaming of an age of unrestricted viewing. As a child, one particular event stood out as having a guiding influence towards healthy scepticism. On a summer family trip to a Devon fishing village we were walking along the coastline when an inexplicable chill caught me off guard. It was only later, whilst exploring the local tourist office, that I realized the coastal cave that I had been walking by had probably housed a cannibalistic family centuries before. Had it been a sign of some paranormal connection? The question led me on a sceptical path. I immediately examined all the possible explanations, even the paranormal ones. I found the process of searching as exciting as the possible answers.

My beliefs at this early age definitely leaned towards the paranormal.

It wasn't until I started looking into the subject, examining the evidence, reading scientific research, that I realized there was a veritable bounty of explanations out there. I'm reminded of the phrase "The Truth is Out There"! I even took a brief foray into the world of tarot and rune-stone readings and found that even when I gave friends an exact opposite reading to the one I was instructed to give, they were amazed. Despite walking an unpopular path of scepticism, I remained empathic to others' paranormal experiences. Even whilst studying for a PhD in Parapsychology, after almost 15 years being fascinated by, and entrenched in, the subject, I still never tired of hearing experiences. This was helped, in no small part, by my third year undergraduate project that examined the relationship between paranormal beliefs and experiences. The relationship is an eternal 'chicken or egg' dilemma. By this I mean, are beliefs in the paranormal as a result of experiences, or are the experiences interpreted as paranormal because of a prior belief? I'm still searching for the answer, but I've encountered examples of both. I'll share some of them with you later. It's when I listen to these examples that I smile at how lucky I am to be involved in an area that means so much to so many people.

The Clairvoyant - Billy Roberts

Having been mediumistically inclined since I was a child, it is very difficult for me to offer an opinion of what it is like not to have any psychic skills at all. From as far back as I can recall, seeing so-called 'dead' people was commonplace to me, and there was a time when I really thought that everyone was the same as me. Once I had reached my teens I began to quickly realize that these 'unusual' abilities, I had always experienced, were in fact not normal. I wish I could say that my encounters with the 'dead' had never presented any problems, but I cannot, because they did. As a child I was extremely introverted, shy and very insecure. The fact that I spent most of my childhood in hospital, as a consequence of poor health, I suppose did not help. And so I always felt peculiarly different from other children, and possessed a strong sense that I had somehow been born in the wrong place at the wrong time.

Sometime around the age of nine, it was suggested to my parents that I should see a child psychologist. They knew that I was psychologically normal, but there was a suspicion that there was something wrong at a deeper, more subtle level. I was subjected to the usual psychological tests, which I thought quite fun; coloured pictures with abstract scenes, geometric puzzles and other strange shapes, that I had to carefully study and say what I could see. The whole consultation lasted around an hour, at the end of which I was given a packet of sweets and a pat on the head, and told how clever I was. The psychologist's report concluded that I was extremely sensitive, creative with a vivid imagination, and that my psychological and emotional development had been inhibited as a consequence of being frequently hospitalized. I later discovered though that the psychologist had completely misunderstood my psychic experiences, and had said that they were totally outside the parameters of traditional science. No prognosis was made and nothing further was done. I was left to my own devices and, although my mother understood the things I experienced, even she wondered how it would affect me in later life.

I have no doubt whatsoever that children who possess paranormal or mediumistic abilities, are super-sensitive in every way possible. The psychic child is very often extremely nervous and insecure. In fact, although most children daydream, or fix their stare on an empty point in space, psychic children do this quite a lot. Any attempt to interrupt their stare causes overwhelming anxiety similar to that experienced when woken from a deep sleep. My mother always allowed me to daydream, and only became concerned about my psychological state when I began to sleepwalk. In fact, sleepwalking was quite a problem for me for some years, and I wouldn't sleep without a nightlight in my bedroom. The one thing my mother never did was encourage me to relate my psychic experiences to her. This, too, is extremely unhealthy and detrimental to the child's emotional and psychological health.

By the time I was ten years old my interest in music had really grown and, for some reason, my psychic tendencies were gradually channelled into the creative areas of my life. Everything changed dramatically, and although my psychic skills were still there, they had somehow become compartmentalized into the subconscious parts of my mind. At that time I slept with my guitar, and would play it every spare moment. In fact, the guitar was my best friend and I really didn't want anyone else. By then I was psychically attuned to a creative life and wanted nothing else. I know now that in the early years of my life I was somehow preoccupied with my paranormal surroundings, and seeing 'dead' people was commonplace to me and a very natural part of my life. Primarily because my life as a musician between the ages of 16 and 24 was extremely exciting and totally took over everything I did, the paranormal side of my life had been compartmentalized to be called upon later. This is not to say that my life was void of paranormal experiences; on the contrary. My psychic abilities were still very much in evidence, but now had taken a back seat, so to speak, and had been channelled into the creative areas of my life.

Our Work
The Clairvoyant - Billy Roberts
Working as a Medium
I suppose it could be said that when I first began working as a medium I was quite naïve. Like most mediums I wanted to serve as many Spiritualist Churches as I could and basically had a strong desire to serve and become known as a good medium. For many years I travelled the UK taking services wherever I was invited. Although it took me some years, I eventually awakened to the fact that it was time to move on and call it a day. However, I did find that the Spiritualist Church circuit was a good training arena, and although I am not one for hymn singing and public prayers, all this did teach me to be disciplined and gave me a sense of responsibility. Because of my more than radical approach to mediumship, I have to admit that some churches did not like the way I worked, particularly the pious and holier than thou churches who were always ready to cast aspersions behind the closed doors of their committee rooms. I had had enough and could see no

point in preaching to the converted or, for that matter, staying where I was not wanted.

In 1982 I founded The Thought Workshop, the North West's first Centre for Psychic and Spiritual Studies and Alternative Therapies. This was an innovation but was greatly opposed by many Spiritualist churches, particularly churches operating under the auspices of the SNU (The Spiritualists National Union), who suggested that I was setting up in opposition to them. This was quite ridiculous. It had been my intention and sincere hope that The Thought Workshop would attract people from all over the UK who wanted to train to be mediums or healers, without all the religious trappings. The centre welcomed some of the most knowledgeable esoteric speakers in the country, and it also gave me the opportunity and privilege to meet many veterans of Spiritualism and the best exponents of the mediumistic profession. This was where I was fortunate enough to meet Ursula Roberts, a world-renowned speaker and deep trance medium, through whom the great Ramadan spoke. Although I had seen many trance mediums before, Ursula Roberts was quite special and someone for whom I had always had the greatest of the respect. As well as being an incredible trance medium, Ursula Roberts was also an author with innumerable books to her credit. Whilst Ursula was in trance, Ramadan spoke to me about my future work. During the sitting I was given a message from my father who had passed away in 1970. He spoke about my mother's illness, and said that she would soon join him. Nobody knew that my mother was dying with lung cancer. Both my father's and mother's names were given, along with other personal details about my family and I. This was probably one of the most incredible mediumistic experiences I have ever had.

Ivor James - a mentor and a psychic artist
During my work as a medium, no one has helped me more than psychic artist, Ivor James (now deceased). In fact, he was far more than a psychic artist; he was extremely knowledgeable and known internationally for his 'Wisdom Teachings', which could be obtained on audio

cassette. Ivor and his wife Marjory visited The Thought Workshop on numerous occasions. Primarily because the centre was struggling financially, Ivor very rarely accepted a fee for his work and was always quite happy just to receive his travelling costs. His audiences were always enthralled with the detail of his sketches, and would always be fascinated when he produced the finished drawing of a 'dead' relative, friend or even a Spirit Guide. Unlike many other psychic artists, Ivor always refused to use an overhead projector, preferring to sit quietly sketching, occasionally muttering his humorous dialogue, which always kept the audience entertained.

I once asked Ivor if he actually saw the people he was drawing, and said that he simply felt them intuitively, and sometimes glimpsed them in his mind's eye. Although in my opinion Ivor James was most probably one of the world's best exponents of psychic art, there have been, and still are, many others. Coral Polge was also an incredible psychic artist. Unlike Ivor, who sketched with a pencil, Coral always worked with coloured pastels and also used an overhead projector so that her magnificent portraits could be seen by the entire audience. Coral was also an excellent exponent of clairvoyance and always accompanied her sketches with evidential mediumistic information.

Unlike other mediums, psychic artists are extremely visual and are able to draw the likeness of the communicating spirit. Although most psychic artists nearly always announce that their drawings are not photographic likenesses, both Ivor's and Coral's sketches were very often like photographs and always magnificent works of art.

Even today I find working as a medium very depleting, and mentally draining. However, I am not too sure whether this has anything to do with my general health, or whether it's a state of health all mediums experience. In my early years I really enjoyed the work; however, today I find it an extremely arduous task, particularly when things have not gone too well, mediumistically speaking. The higher the profile, the more people expect from a medium. It is an extremely responsible profession as I always feel that I am playing with people's emotions. I am quite sure that sometimes a medium can do more damage than good, and even with the best intentions, positive results cannot in anyway be guaranteed.

For me personally, the most frustrating thing about working mediumistically is its inconsistency. Even when a medium is feeling quite positive about his or her communication, the process can seem confused and somewhat incoherent. This is quite often the result of negativity created by the audience, which can have a profound effect upon the whole process of mediumship. When this happens during my theatre demonstrations I have to switch from working mediumistically to working psychically. Less effort is required with this process, and because it is also much quicker, I am then able to speak to far more people than I would using my mediumistic skills. I always feel that whilst mediumship works primarily within the confines of my brain, psychic skills function within the solar plexus. Of course, this is not entirely true as both processes take place within the extremely complex structures of both the nervous system and the brain. This is the reason why the whole process of a mediumistic demonstration can be mentally depleting. I always feel it the following day and find it very difficult to concentrate or motivate myself. In all the years of working as a medium I have never found a solution to this. Although all mediums are different, the effects of working mediumistically are the same for everyone. All mediums are psychic but not all psychics are mediums; a medium's brain functions in a slightly different way, enabling it to receive data on a completely different frequency. For me personally, the 'tuning-in' process, before I demonstrate my mediumistic skills, is literally like flicking through the dial on a radio. It may take me sometime before the correct frequency is located, and even when it is, it may not be as clear and distinct as I would like it to be. I am not making excuses for myself; I am simply stating a fact. This is why mediumistic demonstrations are inconsistent and very unreliable, and the primary reason why parapsychologists are able to criticize it and present the scientific reasons why it is not possible to communicate with the so-called 'dead'.

The Parapsychologist - Ciarán O'Keeffe
Working as a Scientist

There's a quote by a French mathematician/philosopher of science, Henri Poincaré, which I like to give to people questioning my interest in science:

> "Science is built up of facts, as a house is built of stones; but an accumulation of facts is no more a science than a heap of stones is a house."

It's true; science is built up of facts, but understanding those facts and actually investigating the truth behind those facts, is what I'm interested in. I don't want to 'merely accumulate facts', I want to investigative them for myself and I want to give others the facts, and let them decide. This is what happens on any given day.

Metaphorically speaking I wear many hats. When I'm wearing my 'academic' hat you'll sometimes find me in my office. The rest of the time I may be discussing research with a colleague or standing in front of a class of students delivering a lecture on a number of aspects of psychology - statistics, forensic psychology, investigative psychology, victimology, music psychology, psychophysics and, of course, parapsychology. Though there is occasional apathy and laziness from students, the rewards come from getting through to even one student in an entire semester. When you, as a lecturer, see the eyes of a student widen as something suddenly clicks in their brain as you tell them about experimental method, all the long hours become worth it. It's not the only way I impart knowledge. I also occasionally have dissertation students who study anything from Forensic Psychology to Parapsychology. I always smile when one of these students comes into my office and looks at my book collection - the nineteenth century collections of eyewitness accounts, the early Parapsychology texts, the hundreds of books on the wackiest fringe subjects (UFOs, Atlantis, Cults, Cryptozoology and the like). But why is this huge collection of books necessary? And, as all my students say - "Have you read all of these?"

I've grown up fascinated by wild and wacky things. I've read a lot, but, more importantly, and this is where I get serious, I've grown into a critical thinker and a scientific sceptic. Scientific scepticism should be a truly open-minded position in which one questions the veracity of claims lacking empirical evidence (i.e. not derived from experimentation and observation) whilst 'critical thinking' is reflective thinking involving the evaluation of evidence relevant to a claim so that a sound conclusion can be drawn (from the evidence). In other words, I don't accept claims based on faith, anecdotes, belief or unfalsifiable hypotheses. An unfalsifiable hypothesis means something that cannot be proved or disproved, for example, that there is life after death. I like to think I'm in a state of perpetual inquiry and perhaps more of a pyrrhonist sceptic (if there are any philosophers reading you'll know what I mean). As a critical thinker there are certain basics to assessing a claim -

1. What claim is being made?
2. What evidence is being presented?
3. Does the evidence support the claim being made?
4. Are there better claims to be made on the same evidence?

I think about this process of thought when I'm confronted with a medium claimant. The medium is claiming they can communicate with the dead (1), they either present a reading to me or testimonials from previous clients (2), I make a decision on whether the evidence points to the possibility of spirit communication (3), or whether there are alternative explanations for what I'm hearing (4). At the same time I assess whether the evidence is acceptable (i.e. is it solely based on faith or anecdotes or is unfalsifiable). I greatly admire the work and writings of Marcello Truzzi (a fellow pyrrhonist), who founded the Society for Scientific Exploration, the Center for Scientific Anomalies Research and who was a founding co-chairman of the Committee for the Scientific Investigation of Claims of the Paranormal (CSICOP - now known as CSI, the Committee for Skeptical Inquiry). It was his original quote, "Extraordinary claims require extraordinary proof", which has been frequently paraphrased and hijacked by the sceptical, and some would argue, cynical community (a quote that itself grew out of Hume's quote "A wise man...proportions his belief to the evidence"). Here are Marcello Truzzi's original thoughts about scepticism (or 'skepticism' in the US) and the place where the idea for the aforementioned quote grew out of.

> "In science, the burden of proof falls upon the claimant; and the more extraordinary a claim, the heavier is the burden of proof demanded. The true skeptic takes an agnostic position, one that says the claim is not proved rather than disproved. He asserts that the claimant has not borne the burden of proof and that science must continue to build its cognitive map of reality without incorporating the extraordinary claim as a new "fact." Since the true skeptic does not assert a claim, he has no burden to prove anything. He just goes on using the established theories of "conventional science" as usual. But if a critic asserts that there is evidence for disproof, that he has a negative hypothesis-saying, for instance, that a seeming psi result was actually due to an artifact-he is making a claim and therefore also has to bear a burden of proof."
> - Marcello Truzzi, Zetetic Scholar, #12-13, (1987)

Let's stop being so academic for a bit. Sort out the wood from the trees. That's essentially what I do. Or attempt to do. This isn't a Pagan or camp fire thing I'm talking about. Believe me I learnt all about the significance of trees whilst dating a carefree Pagan in my wild and tempestuous days! No, this is essentially to do with studying psychics and mediums and trying to sort out the good wood from the bad. Try being a parapsychologist who specializes in testing psychics and mediums. The occasional media appearance, newspaper interview or advert in the local press asking for volunteers has my email inbox groaning. I can send you an mp3 of it actually groaning if you like. It means that somehow I have to sort out who are the potentially 'good' psychics and who are the out-and-out fraudsters. Aside from it being extremely difficult, you do have to be really careful. In Maryland a few years ago a resident lost $100,000 after visiting a psychic at a local mall and being told her family was cursed. "She was told the curse was centuries old and she would have to go through a cleansing ritual to be rid of that curse," police spokesperson Lucille Baur said. "She had to cash in savings and bring that currency in for that cleansing ritual." The cleansing ritual cleaned out her savings and that's when she went to the police. It's a bit different in Montgomery County, Maryland though. Fortune-telling is illegal.

There are hundreds of other examples throughout the world. *The Sunday Times* in Australia compiled a report of the ten worst scams of 2005. Two of them referred to psychics:

Maria Rosais: She claims a dark force is stopping you from winning $30,000. Her crystals and precious stones, plus her ritual, will drive it away for a cost of $62.

Blanche Calmette: Blanche tells people something strange is happening and she is anxious to do their astrological chart. For $79.95 you'll get a reading and confirm your address, so it can then be passed on to other 'psychic' sharks.

Is it all doom and gloom? No, but we are constantly confronted with failure and, yet, we must always keep an open mind.

Chapter 2:
Defining the Paranormal

"The weight of evidence for an extraordinary claim must be proportioned to its strangeness."
- Pierre-Simon, Marquis de Laplace [French mathematician and astronomer]

The Parapsychologist - Ciarán O'Keeffe
Parapsychology and the Paranormal

The words 'paranormal' and 'parapsychology' share the prefix 'para' which means, in Latin, 'against, counter, outside or beyond the norm'. Parapsychology is traditionally defined as the scientific study of ESP and PK. PK stands for Psychokinesis and is the alleged ability to move or alter an object through the use of the sixth sense. A good example of this, which I'm sure everybody knows, is the alleged psychokinetic phenomena of spoon-bending. ESP stands for Extra-Sensory Perception and covers *telepathy, precognition and clairvoyance*. These are three alleged processes that rely on information being obtained without the use of any of the known five senses. *Telepathy*, for example, is essentially mind-to-mind communication, *precognition* is future prediction, and clairvoyance is the ability to decipher information about an object (i.e. mind-to-object interaction). Although laboratory tests of clairvoyance focus on a psychic's ability to get details about an object, or drawing, or details about the owner, the most common form of clairvoyance, as defined by parapsychologists, is psychometry.

Psychometry

Imagine the scenario, a team investigating the death of a third victim in a brutal serial killer case call in a psychic to help. The psychic knows no details about the case. He is presented with an object from the crime scene, a knife. The knife is the murder weapon, but because the murderer is forensically aware he wore gloves, and so no DNA evidence can be traced on the weapon. The psychic relaxes for a moment and attempts to divine, or discover, using their psychic ability. He picks up detailed information about the owner of the knife, even transporting himself, for a moment, to a vivid replay of the crime scene. Overcome by the ferocious emotions of the killer, the psychic stops. He has provided enough detail to give the team valuable clues - clues that will hopefully lead to capture, arrest and conviction.

The process that the psychic was going through is termed 'Psychometry'. A term that has been around since the late 1800s, it refers to the ability to obtain information from an object, without the aid of any of one's normal senses. Scientific scrutiny of such ability is almost impossible. Take the knife from the criminal scenario described above. How can we be certain the information the psychic is allegedly picking up is from the murderer? It could be information from the knife's previous owner, or from the shop owner who sold it, or from one of the workers on the factory line that was responsible for its manufacture.

As parapsychologists interested in testing an alleged ability there is only so far we can search when it comes to psychometry. I've conducted tests on psychometrists, ingenious if I do say so myself. I've instructed a colleague to buy five identical items of jewellery and, still wrapped (or untouched in their identical gift boxes), give them to five different people with instructions to wear the jewellery over the Christmas holiday period. Then a psychic, specializing in psychometry, gives readings whilst holding the jewellery. The psychic is unaware of who each item belongs to, including whether they're male or female. In addition, when I interact with the psychic, I'm also ignorant of who the owners are. When all the participants are presented with the readings and asked to choose their own reading none of them are able to do so. If there is anything to the ability, the people taking part should be able to recognize the reading given to them. Unfortunately, it doesn't happen. But, if we were being truly thorough with the investigation we would track down everyone who had come into contact with the jewellery and present them with the readings. Psychometry, therefore, as an ability to be tested, is almost impossible. Mediumship, however, lends itself better to scientific testing.

Mediumship
Defining mediumship is not the easiest task. It's commonly thought of as 'communication with the dead' but, frequently, the word 'dead' is replaced with synonyms such as 'discarnate entities', 'spirit' etc. It comes under the umbrella term of parapsychology because of the communication aspect. The Koestler Parapsychology Unit (in Edinburgh University) defines Parapsychology as "the study of apparent new means of communication, or exchange of influence, between organisms & environment". A medium, receiving messages from spirit, is demonstrating a 'means of communication'.

Mediumship is traditionally studied by psychical investigators rather than parapsychologists. This may be due to the fact that what is considered to be the founding era of spiritualist mediums (i.e. late 1800s, early 1900s), was rife with deception, fraud and sensationalism. Parapsychologists tend to distance themselves from the area of mediumship because of this early controversy and because of it's elusiveness in the laboratory. Mediumship, or communicating with the dead, is traditionally conducted in a séance environment, where, it is argued, the presence of actual sitters assists with the communication. Elsewhere, communication can be achieved in one-to-one settings, on a platform in a Spiritualist Church, or in a theatre. Though there are cases throughout the last century of famous mediums volunteering for laboratory work (e.g. Harry Price's work with Rudi Schneider), the success rate in a highly controlled environment is not high. This may also be because of a number of natural explanations for what a medium produces. During a traditional reading with a medium, the medium usually produces a large number of statements and the sitter has to decide whether these statements accurately describe departed loved ones or relatives. It is widely recognized that the sitter's endorsement of such statements cannot be taken as evidence of mediumistic ability, as seemingly accurate readings can be created by a set of psychological stratagems collectively referred to as 'cold reading'. It is therefore vital that any investigation into the possible existence of mediumistic ability prevents any of these stratagems from being used. We discuss mediumship in greater detail in Chapter 3 when Billy introduces his experiences with this method of communication.

The Clairvoyant - Billy Roberts

It must be understood that not all those who are mediumistically gifted are clairvoyant, and not all clairvoyants are mediums. To the layman this may all sound a little confusing, but the truth is that the majority of mediums do not actually 'see', clairvoyantly speaking, at all. I am a clairaudient medium predominantly, and although I do see clairvoyantly, I have found that this skill is not consistent and, more often than not, does not work simultaneously with my clairaudience.

Clairaudience is the ability to 'hear' super-sensual sounds. When I hear a spirit voice it is a voice, often extremely clear, and usually coming into my brain from the left side of my head. The phenomenon of clairaudience is probably the rarest of all mediumistic skills and, in many ways, the most detrimental to psychological health. Sometimes the phenomenon of clairaudience is no more than an extraneous thought, entering the brain, and then manifesting as sound in the auditory system. Sometimes when I am working with a theatre audience, I don't have time to analyse the individual senses and, more often than not I receive the information, collectively, via all my psychic skills.

Clairvoyance is perhaps the most familiar word relating to psychic abilities. The majority of people know exactly what a clairvoyant is. This is the ability to 'see' things the ordinary person cannot. When a clairvoyant possesses mediumistic skills he or she is able to see images of the deceased. These images may appear as minute nebulous forms inside the medium's head, or it may be the individual standing there as solidly as everyone else. Without the ability to 'hear' spirit voices, the information received by a clairvoyant medium is sometimes quite limited. Additional information about the spirit communicator is obtained through the medium's ability to sense. This skill is called *Clairsentience* and is one that is possessed by most people, mediumistic or not. Clairsentience is very often greatly underestimated, as the information obtained by a clairsentient medium can be quite specific. Through clairsentience a medium is often able to give a detailed description of the spirit communicator with a name, how the person died and even where he or she lived. I possess all three mediumistic skills, but unfortunately for me they do not always work simultaneously, and quite often I find myself only using my clairsentient skill. I am quite certain that this is the reason why mediumistic demonstrations are not consistent, and also why a lot of the information mediumistically obtained is quite vague and seemingly incoherent.

Psychometry is a psychic process that is greatly misunderstood by most people. Although a lot of mediums use Psychometry when giving readings, technically it is purely a psychic skill and not a mediumistic one. For the uninitiated, Psychometry is the process of gently handling a small artefact, such as a ring or watch, until the mind is impressed with images and feelings relating to those to whom the article has belonged. The misconception is that Psychometry is a direct link to a deceased person, and this is not so. Psychometry is a method of mentally processing information relating to the history of the artefact. For example, where it was bought, by whom, and was it bought for a special occasion. Names are also frequently obtained through this process. In other words, Psychometry is the process of mentally analysing data and in theory may only connect the medium's mind with the past and present history of the artefact. However, whilst psychometerising an article the medium often makes a connection with a deceased person and is then able to obtain further information from another source. The artefact has only helped to relax the medium's mind allowing other mediumistic skills to operate.

Although Psychometry has never really been my forte, I do occasionally use it as a process for training my mind. In fact

Psychometry is an ideal tool for cultivating the senses and developing Clairvoyant skills, and it is an exercise I always recommend to developing mediums.

At this point I would like to clarify the difference between information 'psychically obtained', as opposed to 'mediumistically obtained'. When a medium is not able to obtain information from a deceased person and is not working with the spirit world, he or she has to then rely solely upon the psychic senses, through which information is obtained primarily about the person's life, past, present and future.

Chapter 3: Mediumship & Communicating with Spirit

The Clairvoyant - Billy Roberts

Working as a professional medium for over 25 years I have come to the conclusion that mediumship is inconsistent and extremely unreliable. Results cannot be guaranteed as the whole phenomenon of mediumship is experimental and does not always work. When I am working mediumistically I very often have no control over the process of receiving information from the spirit world. I frequently feel so frustrated when a bereaved person visits me to make contact with a loved one without success. Before beginning a consultation I always explain that a medium cannot call anyone back from the spirit world, and that I have no control whatsoever over the process of communication. All that I am able to do is mentally request that the person the sitter wants to hear from will come close to me. This is all I am able to do. I always use the analogy of a telephone exchange, and explain that a medium's mind is like that and that the spirit world makes contact with me and not the other way round. Because mediumship does not always work, and a medium cannot be selective where their spirit communicators are concerned, occasionally those who consult mediums for consolation and comfort leave feeling worse than when they came in. For this reason I often feel very uncomfortable about the whole process of mediumship and wonder if it is somewhat distasteful, and at worst, immoral.

As all mediums are different, I can really only speak for myself regarding how I feel when I am actually working mediumistically. When I am preparing for a demonstration of mediumship, I become extremely agitated and my stomach begins to turn. I usually lose all sense of my surroundings and find myself restlessly pacing the room. All this usually happens at least fifteen minutes before I walk on stage, and I also become overwhelmed with a strange feeling of 'not being there'.

Although I define myself as a 'Clairaudient' medium, that is one who 'hears', I am also clairvoyant and clairsentient, and am able to 'see' and 'sense' discarnate beings. To the layman all this may sound a little far-fetched and fanciful, but, when I am on stage and demonstrating my mediumistic skills, it is literally like having a radio inside my head and, until a communication with a deceased person has been made, the tuning dial moves involuntarily from frequency to frequency. This is exactly how it feels to me, and once the 'tuning in' process has been completed, I then hear a disembodied voice. This voice may sometimes sound muffled and incoherent, and other times it may come across as being extremely clear. I must say that I have no control whatsoever over this 'tuning in' process, and once I am out on that stage, I am completely at the mercy of those in the discarnate world of spirit.

Although there are times when the voices I hear are no more than extraneous thoughts being processed through my brain, they are mostly audible sounds, usually coming into the left side of my head. The only way to ascertain whether or not these voices are real is by the content of the information they pass on to me. Sometimes the communicating voice will be quite specific with what it is saying, and other times it will sound incoherent, vague and somewhat confused. When the communicator is quite strong, the information is clear and will direct me to exactly where the message is to be given. By specific, I mean the first and second names either of the communicating spirit, or of the person to whom the message is given. The vague messages are usually descriptions that could apply to almost anyone.

After a mediumistic demonstration I always know when I have had a successful show and received evidential information from a genuine discarnate source. The adrenalin rush causes me to feel quite 'high', and I remain in this state for several hours and find it quite difficult to sleep.

Telepathy or Talking to the Dead?
The most frequently asked question is: 'Do mediums really talk to discarnate souls, or is it some form of telepathy?' There is really no direct and simple way of answering this question. To begin with though, the fundamental principle underlying every mediumistic process is telepathy. This is mind-to-mind communication, albeit a process involving a discarnate mind with an incarnate mind. But it still involves the process of telepathy. However, regardless of the accuracy of information given by a medium, all that it proves is that the medium has an ability the majority of people do not have. The method used to process information in the medium's brain is purely subjective, and so the medium alone knows whether the information he or she is receiving actually originates from a discarnate source. A medium's job is to endeavour to prove that life continues beyond death, and the only way in which this can be successfully achieved is by passing on information, of an extremely personal nature, from a deceased friend or relative. I suppose it could be said that when a medium is working, he or she unknowingly accesses some sort of super-sensual memory bank and that the connection between the medium's brain and this memory bank is possibly achieved by the person for whom the information is intended, and not the medium at all. Although quite a complex concept, I suppose it is quite feasible. I do accept the fact that such a super-sensual memory banking system does exist, and that there is an electro-magnetic substance in the ether capable of recording every event, thought and emotion. However, that does not explain why some mediums can have a two-way conversation with a disembodied soul, and why information can be given, about which the person to whom the medium is speaking, has no knowledge whatsoever. If such a two-way conversation does take place, then this would suggest that there is intelligence behind the disembodied source.

Firstly, it must be understood that the whole process of mediumship is experimental and does not always work. Because of its very nature it is an extremely unreliable process, dependent upon certain things.

(1) Conducive conditions of the place in which the mediumistic demonstration takes place. (2) The mental, emotional and physical states of the medium. (3) The attitudes of those to whom messages are given. (4) Last but by no means least, whether or not the discarnate beings want to communicate with the medium. The majority of people would find the last statement a little difficult to accept. However, not all discarnate beings want to communicate, just as not all incarnate beings want to talk. A medium has no control over the process of communication and cannot command spirits to return. The other fallacy is that people dramatically change once they have made the transition from this world to the next. This is not true! An alcoholic or drug addict who has not achieved a cure before they pass to the spirit world still has to address their addictions. The only difference is that they no longer have access to alcohol or drugs. However, they do have access to the minds of those still incarnated in the physical world. Those with bad habits in this world are easy prey for those in the lower spheres of the spirit world who desperately need to feed their habits.

Occasionally when I am demonstrating my mediumistic skills in a theatre I find myself having to deal with an unpleasant spirit endeavouring to infiltrate my energy field. Although I can usually cope with such offensive entities, there has been the odd occasion when I have had to make my excuses and leave the stage. In fact, this has happened to me twice in over 25 years. On both occasions I have been feeling a little under the weather, and this seemed to be the reason why the entity was able to gain access to my aura. On each occasion I was violently sick with an overwhelming feeling of disorientation. On one of the occasions I actually lost consciousness for a few minutes and was taken into the dressing room to recover. When I came round I had no recollection of what had happened, but felt as though my head had been used as a football. These experiences made me realize that as well as occasionally working with so-called 'Angelic Forces', a medium must always be prepared for the unexpected. There are vagabonds in the lower spheres of the spirit world whose sole intention is to prevent light from entering into this world. Primarily because of their psychic make-up, and the fact that they are channels, mediums are extremely vulnerable and prime targets for these entities. To prevent such attacks mediums have to be psychologically strong and emotionally stable. Because the whole process of mediumship has a profound effect upon the emotions and psychological nature, unless the medium is well ground, psychologically speaking, then such psychic infiltrations are unavoidable. I am quite certain that this is the reason why the majority of mediums are unhealthy. In order to maintain a healthy body and mind, training is paramount where the cultivation of mediumistic skills are concerned.

Implications of Mediumship

It is really only over the past ten years that I have come to realize that mediumistic skills are totally unreliable, and that the whole process of the mediumistic phenomenon is wholly dependent upon the medium's physical as well as his or her psychological well-being. What really concerns me, however, is the profound effect that the use of mediumistic abilities has upon the psychological status of the medium, and the sometimes even greater effect it has upon the minds and emotions of those who consult mediums and clairvoyants. Although I do not agree with the harsh Biblical warnings about consulting mediums, I have in recent years come to the conclusion that some of those who consult mediums are, in many ways, emotionally damaged as a consequence. The observations I have made during my 26 or so years as a professional medium, have now led me to conclude that not all mediums are genuine, and even those who are not genuine, are still able to somehow produce an incredible effect upon the lives of those who consult them. This is a frightening thought and has made me seriously reconsider the whole concept of my own mediumistic skills. I know only too well when it works for me, and I equally know when it does not. I can also see when a so-called medium is NOT genuine, and when he or she is demonstrating what has become known as 'cold reading'. I am not too sure that this is the correct term to use when describing someone who is employing other than psychic means to give a reading. I am quite certain that even the non-psychic person uses intuition when endeavouring to give a reading. Combined with other psychological observations, some so-called psychics are able to produce remarkable results. However, whether or not these results can be defined as 'genuine' is perhaps somewhat debatable, and will be explored later on.

First of all, no special credentials or qualifications are legally required for one to begin working as a medium or clairvoyant. Anyone can create a business as a clairvoyant, and as a result, make a reasonable living. I suppose this is exactly the reason why I now find it all a little distasteful and, at times, somewhat immoral.

Having made a detailed analysis of mediumship and the different ways in which mediums demonstrate their skills, I have compiled a list of mediumistic techniques and styles to enable comparisons to be drawn when making your final assessment.

1. PSYCHIC COUNSELLING MEDIUMS: Mediumistic messages with no evidential content, simply offering counselling of a spiritual and emotional nature. The usual being, 'By June everything will be alright, and then there will be a new beginning.' Etc, etc.

2. SUPERFICIAL INFORMATION MEDIUMS: This covers quite a broad spectrum where mediumistic messages are concerned, and can range from the general terminology used by a lot of mediums, such as "I have a motherly figure here," meaning mother, grandmother or someone like a mother, to the proverbial man in a uniform or naval condition. Then we have the common and very often general names given by mediums. These are usually the popular names of the city or town. Names peculiar to the northern parts of England, for example, are remarkably different to the names of those who live in the south. Read on...

3. PERSONALITY MEDIUMS: I define these as the mediums who are

very popular and liked by everyone. Unfortunately, these sorts of mediums are usually liked for the wrong reasons, and very often have a large following because of their personality and performance. They are usually entertaining and know exactly how to handle an audience and hold attention. Those who consult 'Personality mediums' are very often blinded by them and fail to see the lack of substance in what they are saying. These sorts of mediums usually have quite a large following. The majority of people seem to think that if a medium is on television and is famous that they are genuine and good. This is not necessarily true.

4. PSYCHOLOGICAL PROFILING MEDIUMS: These are those mediums and clairvoyants who have become quite adept at reading the psychological profiles of those who consult them. They instinctively know what the person wants to hear, by the sound of the voice, facial expressions and overall body language. In fact, they become attuned to the individual's needs very quickly. In other words, they have learnt to read their clients like books. However, it must be said that this technique is second nature to them and so they are not always aware of what they are doing.

5. TRANCE AND OVERSHADOWED MEDIUMS: These are mediums who find it easier to hide behind a self-created personality of a so-called 'dead' individual. Although genuine trance mediums most certainly do exist, these are few and far between. They are in a minority, and the majority of what purports to be trance is no more than a brazen attempt to deceive those with a genuine interest in the subject. Mostly, though, those who believe they are working in trance are self-deluded, and very often truly believe in what they are doing.

6. THE NAMES MEDIUM: Although their styles vary considerably, these types of mediums give nothing but lots of names to their recipients, with no other information. Quite often the person is not given the opportunity to respond, and so onlookers are left wondering whether

the names have been accepted or not.

7. TRAVELLING MEDIUMS: Unless a medium is genuine, one often finds that his or her mediumistic skills do not work as efficiently outside of their own town. As I have said previously, names and environmental situations in the south of England, for example, are completely different to those in the north.

8. HIT AND MISS MEDIUMS: This style of mediumship involves throwing out as much information as possible until things are accepted.

It must be borne in mind, however, that even those mediums who are not genuine very often believe that they are. Whether or not this is down to training or, to the lack of it, I am not too sure. However, the Spiritualist Church circuit is full of self-deluded people who genuinely believe that they are mediums and are able to receive messages from the 'Spirit World'. In many ways, though, the fault must lie with those who consult mediums. For those who consult mediums very often have nothing else with which to make a comparison, and so, the vague and superficial information sometimes given by mediums is very often exaggerated and blown completely out of all proportion. A medium is only as good as those to whom the messages are given. Should the recipient of a medium's message respond enthusiastically, then the medium is bound to be overwhelmed with a sense of satisfaction and achievement. All this gives an incredible boost to the confidence of the medium, making them believe even more in his or her mediumistic ability.

The Debunkers

I once saw a television programme in the seventies on which the television mentalist 'The Great Kreskin' interviewed medium, Doris Stokes. He invited her to demonstrate her mediumistic skills to a capacity studio audience, after which he endeavoured to replicate the same. Where Doris Stokes occasionally struggled to place her information, Kreskin gave an extremely impressive demonstration, and gave specifically detailed messages to selected members of the audience. Although Kreskin admitted that his demonstration had been complete fabrication, he would not reveal exactly how it had been done. He did, however, deny that he had 'plants' in the audience. Kreskin rejected any suggestion that he himself was mediumistically inclined and left the studio audience and the viewers completely mystified.

The magician, James Randi, has also demonstrated on numerous occasions that he is able to replicate anything a medium can do, and has even offered a large sum of money to any medium who can prove that he or she possesses even a rudimentary form of paranormal ability. The magician David Burglass has also proved on many occasions that he is able to replicate the skills of any 'so-called mediums'. If a medium's skills can be successfully replicated in this way, shouldn't the general public be more aware of the way in which mediums work? Nineteenth-century Mnemonic expert, Sambrook, devoted a whole chapter in one of his earlier books to *clairvoyance*, explaining how the skill may be successfully achieved with the use of articulated sounds which, Sambrook states, can reveal a broad spectrum of information to the alleged clairvoyant. Of course, with Sambrook's methods this particular technique of *clairvoyance* or *mind reading* will only work with a co-operator. He goes on to explain that in other feats of clairvoyance the Rules of Sounds are equally effective and useful. It's clear that Victorian clairvoyants were most definitely capable of trickery to obtain successful results, and today I am quite certain that the methods employed by some so-called clairvoyants are more elaborately refined and certainly far more polished. Mediumship is a subjective process, and one in which only the mediums themselves know if the information they are giving is genuine or not.

Cold Reading

The term 'cold reading' is extremely out of date now and should no longer be used. Anyway, the term is totally misleading and was most probably created by someone who had no experience whatsoever of genuine mediums. I have appeared on numerous television programmes with professional sceptics, whose cries were always the same, "It's cold reading. Anyone can do that." In fact, it is probably far easier to discredit a medium's work than it is to prove that he or she is genuine. The so-called cold reading technique is used to describe the vague and very general information that could apply to anyone. What sceptics fail to understand is that this theory is brought down when a medium gives detailed information to a recipient. I am talking about specific and extremely detailed information about a deceased relative; description, name and sometimes even the address where he or she lived. This kind of information can hardly be described as 'cold reading', and is a demonstration of genuine mediumship.

The Parapsychologist - Ciarán O'Keeffe

I'm frequently asked why I bother "investigating the paranormal" or even "having anything to do with mediums" if I'm always such a vocal "sceptic in the media!" In addition, you'll already have noted my comments earlier about the general avoidance of mediumship by parapsychologists. For those who read some of my work, or follow what I say quite carefully, you'll already have realized that I am quite open-minded about the field and the special claimants (e.g. psychics, mediums) who litter it. But, it's still a valid question. Why are parapsychologists interested in mediums? And, I believe, there's a valid, and simple, answer.

Some individuals claim to possess mediumistic abilities that allow them to contact the 'spirit world' and receive information from the deceased. There are several reasons to investigate these claims:

First, mediumistic abilities, if valid, would provide evidence to support the survival of bodily death, and thus have important implications for aspects of psychology. Such data would, for example, present a strong challenge to key assumptions underlying neuropsychological research, including the notion that human personality, cognition, and consciousness is dependent on a living brain. Evidence of genuine mediumistic abilities would also raise intriguing questions about the sensory mechanisms that might underlie such abilities and, on a more practical level, have important implications for the many aspects of clinical and counselling psychology concerned with bereavement and grief.

Second, demonstrations of apparent mediumistic abilities have a significant impact on public belief and behaviour. Recent opinion polls have revealed that almost 30 per cent of Americans now believe in the existence of genuine mediumistic abilities, approximately ten per cent of Britons visit mediums to both receive messages from the deceased and obtain general guidance for their lives, and new types of television programmes featuring such demonstrations consistently attract millions of viewers (guilty your honour!). Well-controlled tests of mediums would help the public and television programme makers assess the validity of such alleged abilities, and thus help inform their resulting decisions and behaviour.

Third, certain individuals working in non-paranormal contexts make claims that are analogous to those made by mediums, and the methods developed to test mediums could be used to examine these claims. For example, some clinicians claim to be able to gain insights into patients' backgrounds purely from their reactions to certain projective tests, some practitioners working in an occupational setting appear to be able to give detailed accounts of people's personality simply from their scores on certain assessment tools, and some individuals operating in a forensic context claim to be able to produce accurate profiles of offenders from a very limited amount of behavioural information. Several writers have recently noted that the anecdotal evidence supporting these claims may be the result of the same type of psychology that can underlie the apparent accuracy of mediumistic readings (i.e. the use of general statements, chance, etc), and thus the methods developed to examine such claims may benefit from a thorough understanding of the procedures used to test mediumship.

Given the nature of the theoretical and practical issues surrounding this topic, it is perhaps not surprising that the scientific testing of mediumship has a long and controversial history going back over 100 years and that several parapsychologists are still "having anything to do with mediums!"

Hundreds of studies conducted by members of early psychical societies (namely the Society for Psychical Research and its American counterpart, the ASPR) focused on testing mediums. For many early researchers, questions regarding the assessment of mediumship not only focused on testing a professed ability, but also tackled a much wider issue, the question of human survival of death. Prior to quantitative studies resembling some sort of standard protocol and analytical approach the number of works devoted to mediumship, and therefore *Survival*, research numbered into the thousands.

The wealth of these early studies are purely descriptive, primarily the experimenter's subjective assessment of readings given in séance scenarios during which the experimenter would be present. In these situations the experimenter would often be the target person, and little effort would be made to prevent the medium divining information via alternative means. Later attempts to restrict these alternative explanations for apparent communication success (i.e. evidence of ADC or After Death Communication) resulted in the rather simplistic, yet ingenuous, addition of an 'environmental' control, a control which ensured no normal communication between medium and client. This use of partitions, then later implementation of separate rooms, guaranteed little or no sensory leakage. Certainly rooms, guarded and separated by more than one wall (ideally completely sound-proofed), make any experimentally substantiated claims of mediumship more valid. But what do I mean by the terms 'sensory leakage' or 'cold reading'? Sensory leakage is easier to understand as it simply refers to the medium obtaining information through any of their normal senses (e.g. hearing the client talking and hence deciphering whether they are male or female). 'Cold reading' is a little bit more detailed.

Cold Reading

This is a term that I will constantly refer to during the course of this dialogue, so let me introduce it quickly here. It's also the annoyance of any medium's career since sceptics such as myself frequently put it forward as a possible explanation for a successful reading. Cold reading is a procedure by which the client or audience is persuaded of a 'performer's' apparent psychic ability, through the revealing of their personality and problems. At one extreme, the effectiveness of *cold reading* can be accomplished by delivering a stock spiel, almost like a prepared script full of high probability statements that differ depending on the age, social class or gender of the client. These high probability statements are disguised to appear as though they are obtained through some extraordinary means. Additionally, *cold reading* provides loads of information for the client to actively interpret. Guides on *cold reading* recommend using vagueness and ambiguity within a reading to ensure the willing involvement of the client in its interpretation.

> ...once the client is actively engaged in trying to make sense of the series of sometimes contradictory statements issuing from the reader, he becomes a creative problem solver trying to find coherence and meaning in the total set of statements.
> - (Hyman, 1989, p. 92)

Hyman's original article, considered by many to be the catalyst for cold reading to enter everyday language, acts almost as a manual for potential pseudo-psychic performers. In the article, the key element to cold reading, aside from the Barnum effect which I'll touch upon later, is providing information through cues given by the client. Robert Hicks, a criminal justice analyst and police specialist with the Virginia Department of Criminal Justice, who has an interest in psychic sleuths, noted of many of them that "the psychic becomes attuned to the officer's behaviour and is using the officer's cues the detective leaning forward or raising an eyebrow - to figure out things that haven't been released to the public". Psychics may use standard psychological techniques: their intelligence, deductive reasoning, examining the client and making careful observations. Think of Sherlock Holmes and his amazing powers of observation. I'm not suggesting that psychics and mediums are all fabulous detectives, but if a single medium interacts with hundreds and hundreds of clients over the years there may be observable common trends. If similar questions are asked by similar people with similar backgrounds, worries, dreams etc, then the next 'similar' one that comes through the door is easy prey (for want of a better phrase). Indeed, researchers actually suggest the cold reader uses sharp observation of different clues provided by the client: the clothing, physical features, jewellery, manner of speech, accent, gestures, eye contact, bodily reaction etc.

The information provided by the clues is given back to the client in the form of a reading. The way the information is delivered convinces the listener of its apparent accuracy, makes it more engaging, and is an essential starting point in understanding the techniques paranormal advisors may use. In my opinion, cold reading is only one alternative explanation for why readings appear more accurate than they actually are.

The Rhetoric of Mediumship

My experience with mediumship readings has led me to the opinion that in the majority of cases we're dealing with the power of persuasion, simply rhetoric. Classical rhetoric was associated primarily with persuasive discourse. The purpose of rhetoric was to convince or persuade audiences. Aristotle defined rhetoric as "the faculty of discovering all the available means of persuasion in any given situation". The *New Oxford Dictionary* defines it as, quite simply, "the art of using language effectively to persuade". In mediumship settings, mediums are essentially 'persuading' us that they are a) communicating with the dead and, in most cases, b) that they are more accurate than they actually are.

Aristotle said that we persuade others by three ways: (i) by the appeal to the audience's reason; (ii) by the appeal of the rhetorician's personality or character; (iii) by the appeal to the audience's emotions.

We may use one of these three exclusively or predominantly, or we may use all three. Everyone develops some instincts for adapting these means to fit the subject, occasion, and audience, but by experience and education some people so refine these instincts that their success in dealing with others can be attributed to pure skill, a skill possibly attained by accomplished psychics. Language experts have said that they would expect that as ratings of competence, position in the community and, to a lesser extent, dynamism (energetic personality) increase, the tendency to be persuaded and to comply will increase as well. Think about these three ways that Aristotle talks about the next time you go and see a medium in a theatre.

They are appealing to your reason -
o The medium is apparently obtaining information about someone in the theatre without knowing them.
o They are stating that the information is coming from a paranormal source.
o The medium is presenting themselves as a 'spiritual' person.
o 'Spiritual' people, who have also been given a gift, don't deceive.
o Therefore, they must be communicating with spirit!

They have appeal of personality -
o Is the medium portraying themselves as someone of sound sense, high moral character and kindness?
o Do they relay examples of acts of kindness and sensitivity?
o Do they say something along the lines of "I used to be sceptical"?

They appeal to your emotions-
o Do any of the audience get emotional during the evening?
o Is the evening full of highs and lows?
o Are there moments when the medium lowers his/her voice?
o Are there moments when the medium is silent, apparently listening to something in the air?
o Does the medium make direct eye-to-eye contact with the person he/she is giving the reading to?

Aside from a wealth of work solely on the Barnum Effect (primarily based on personality assessments and objective psychological tests), the lack of investigations into the linguistics and rhetoric of mediumship readings is restricted to mere discussion, and often of only case studies. Despite this, psychological ideas like 'The Barnum Effect' are very effective explanations for what might be happening.

Barnum Effect

Psychologist B. R. Forer found that people tend to accept vague and ambiguous personality descriptions as uniquely applicable to themselves without realizing that the same description could be applied to just about anyone.

How, on earth, could this possibly work, you may ask yourselves? Read the personality description in the box below that I've compiled with the help of a variety of extremely competent psychics. How well does it apply to you?

> *You have a need for other people to like and admire you, and yet you tend to be critical of yourself. While you have some personality weaknesses you are generally able to compensate for them. You have considerable unused capacity that you have not turned to your advantage. Disciplined and self-controlled on the outside, you tend to be worrisome and insecure on the inside. At times you have serious doubts as to whether you have made the right decision or done the right thing. You prefer a certain amount of change and variety and become dissatisfied when hemmed in by restrictions and limitations. You also pride yourself as an independent thinker and do not accept others' statements without satisfactory proof. But you have found it unwise to be too frank in revealing yourself to others. At times you are extroverted, affable, and sociable, while at other times you are introverted, wary, and reserved. Some of your aspirations tend to be rather unrealistic.*

Before I discuss how well the above personality description applies to you, let me tell you a little more about the Barnum Effect. This effect has been given the name 'Forer' or 'Barnum', in deference to circus man P.T. Barnum's reputation as a master psychological manipulator. It is also known as the *subjective validation effect* or the *personal validation effect*. This effect essentially provides the listener with what they want to hear. In 1949, Forer administered the Diagnostic Interest Blank to 39 students in his introductory psychology class. One week later he gave each subject an identical personality description consisting of vague, ambiguous, and general statements, which came largely from a news-stand astrology book. Students were asked to rate the accuracy of their profiles on a scale of 0 (poor) to 5 (perfect). The mean accuracy rating was 4.3. Subsequent studies of the Barnum effect have expanded upon Forer's ideas and questions and have utilized a similar methodological approach. Subjects (a) are administered a personality test, (b) wait while the test is scored, (c) receive a personality profile purportedly derived from the personality test they wrote, and (d) rate the personal accuracy of the profile. In most cases the subjects receive identical personality sketches. So, the personality description I gave you earlier, it's pretty much the same one Forer gave his students over 50 years ago. If you don't think it worked that well, give it to a friend who hasn't read this paragraph. Say that you gave their name to a really good psychic and they came up with this description of them. How impressed are they?

The research indicates agreement that subjects perceive Barnum statements to be accurate descriptions of their personalities. It has been repeatedly demonstrated that general personality profiles supposedly derived from 'psychological assessment' are judged by subjects to be accurate descriptions of themselves. However, some disagreement exists on the reasons for, and factors that affect, the high ratings of acceptance of Barnum profiles. My personal experience is that a level of belief in the paranormal really helps!

Other Problems with Mediumship

What problems could there possibly be with mediumship, an alleged ability that provides a link to departed love ones, or proof of a wonderful life beyond our earthly one? The fact that there are alternative explanations for a medium speaking to the dead means that there is potentially a population of self-deluded mediums out there, or, even worse, a population of frauds. Because, remember, aside from all my academic ramblings about linguistic explanations such cold reading and rhetoric, there is the big four letter 'F' word...Fake! It happens, don't think it doesn't. Don't make the mistake of thinking that fakery and fraud are the arguments of bitter sceptics who haven't had a personal paranormal experience. There are stories out there of mediums who have been caught doing their prior research, eavesdropping on punters' conversations, reusing the same theatre audience members and so on and so on.. We still have to remain sceptical, however, since they are only accounts and only *some* hard concrete evidence exists for fraud. The same for genuine, 100 per cent proof, of spirit communication. Where there's always the possibility of fraud, however, we must be on our guard.

My years of meeting mediums, though, have led me to believe that we're not dealing, in the main, with frauds. Oh, there are definitely frauds selling their wares to unsuspecting people, but I think these frauds give the majority a bad name. I meet mediums who genuinely want to help, who want to understand their ability, who make no great claims. With this majority there are several possibilities for what's going on. They are deceiving me, they are deceiving themselves, or they are genuinely speaking to the dead (or are telepathic!). For those who fit into the 'deception' category there are easily understood explanations for how they appear to get information from an unknown spirit, apart from fraud. These have centred around three key issues: (i) sensory leakage, (ii) the vagueness and ambiguity of the medium's statements and (iii) the impact of sitting face-to-face with a medium (or even face-to-face in a theatre). Remove these issues, test a medium under conditions that satisfy these conditions and if they come up with accurate information then you've come up with the veritable 'white crow' that the famous American psychologist William James sought for. He said "In order to disprove that all crows are black, you need only come up with one white crow."

Chapter 4
Question Time - Part I
The Parapsychologist questions the Clairvoyant - Ciarán asks Billy

Given the emphasis you place on your childhood psychic experiences and comments on children and psychic ability in general, why do you think children are more susceptible to psychic phenomena or communication?
Billy answers: Apart from the extremely significant physiological and psychological reasons, the simplest explanation is that a child's mind is less cluttered, and therefore more susceptible to the influencing energies of the super-sensual universe. Emotionally and psychologically children are more 'in-tune' with the creative force of the universe, and are therefore more able to process these through their image-making faculties. I know all this may sound somewhat far-fetched and fanciful to a scientifically minded person, but without being technical, explaining this is like describing the taste of sugar to someone who has never tasted anything sweet.

Why is your clairvoyant skill not consistent?
Billy answers: Experience has made me realize that no one's clairvoyant skill is consistent. I am quite sure that an awful lot depends on the clairvoyant's moods, emotions and general condition of the health. Let's not forget that psychic and mediumistic skills are in some way connected to the endocrine glands and nerve plexuses, and so the emotional and mental states control the whole process of clairvoyance. Although Clairvoyance is not a normal state of mind, contrary to popular belief, clairvoyants are only human. I defy any clairvoyant to say otherwise.

Can you expand on why clairaudience is detrimental to psychological health?

Billy answers: It is not so much the process of clairaudience that is detrimental to the psychological health, as much as it is its actual development. The cultivation of clairaudience, more than any other mediumistic skill, causes the movement of certain hormones in the body. Should the aspirant either have a history of psychological problems, or a propensity towards them, then the whole psychology of the person may be affected. Even if a psychosis is not precipitated, the mind's equilibrium is greatly affected with the cultivation of clairaudience. As I have previously said, clairaudient mediums often suffer with thyroid problems, diabetes or pancreatic conditions. Even where natural clairaudience is the case, as a consequence of hormonal changes in the body, the medium frequently suffers from depression and all sorts of health problems. Some schools of thought believe that forms of psychotic illnesses cause the sufferer to experience paranormal phenomena at an extremely low level, and that the voices they are said to hear are the voices of a low level of discarnate mind.

For me, as a scientist, I have a real problem in testing 'psychometry' under controlled conditions. Is it difficult to distinguish information from a psychic ability from that obtained by merely looking at an object? (e.g. an item of highly decorative jewellery would probably belong to a lady, its condition could tell you a lot about the person also).

Billy answers: What you are talking about is not psychometry but observation and guess work. Ideally, when testing psychometric skills, the artefact should be concealed in an envelope. This eliminates the possibility of cheating, and encourages the psychic to rely solely upon his or her psychic skills. Psychometry is a specific intuitive skill, through which historical information is gleaned, primarily about the artefact's past and present. This information often includes the owner's relationships, circumstances and past and present situations.

You have mentioned that 15 minutes or so immediately prior to a demonstration of your psychic skills you become agitated and your stomach constantly churns. Isn't that just nerves?
Billy answers: I do agree that these are the symptoms of nerves, and most probably what anyone would experience prior to walking on a stage before an audience. But the agitation and churning stomach experienced by mediums are much more than nerves. I was taught that the spirit world work through the solar plexus, and when that part of the anatomy does not feel unusually agitated then the spirit world is not present.

How can you tell when a 'so-called medium is not genuine'? Do you have to rely on your alleged psychic abilities?
Billy answers: The answer to this question is not as straightforward as it seems. Yes, I do have to use my own psychic abilities, as well as my observation skills as someone who trains mediums. I have been able to physically 'see' the aura since I was a very small child. Over the years I have made a study of this and use it in my work. My observations of the aura enable me to ascertain whether or not the person is actually working with the spirit world, or whether he or she is merely making psychological assessments.

Psychic counselling mediums - Am I right in assuming all messages for this mediumistic style are positive in nature?
Billy answers: Yes and no! Generally speaking this style of mediumship is quite harmless. However, it can also be quite dangerous when one thinks of the immense responsibility all mediums have to those who consult them. The wrong advice or piece of information can be detrimental to a person's life.

Do you see all these mediumistic styles as being fraudulent, issues of self-delusion, or do you think some of these mediums still have an ability? So, where do you fit in all of this?
Billy answers: It would be foolish to suggest that all mediums are frauds - where, then, would that leave me? Of course there are genuine mediums. However, I believe that these are in a minority. I know that this makes me sound somewhat arrogant and perhaps full of my own self-importance. The truth is, though, there are many who should not be working as mediums.

I'm not clear on why you think the term 'cold reading' is out of date?
Billy answers: I've never really been exactly sure what the term 'cold reading' means? This is an Americanism and was originally used to describe a so-called reader who would use certain psychological 'tricks' when giving someone a private consultation. These tricks included observational techniques, such as reading body language, facial expressions, combined with psychological assessments and asking leading questions. As far as I'm concerned this term is way out of date. Most 'readers' have become wise to this term and, as a consequence, have upgraded their techniques and made them a fine art. The term 'cold reading' is not clear and really means nothing quite specific.

Why would mediums resort to plants in the audience, and examining credit details etc?
Billy answers: I have known at least two mediums to involve themselves in this practise, primarily to ensure that the show was successful. I know it goes on today, but I am quite sure that theatre staff would not be a party to this sort of thing. And NO, I have never resorted to such things.

Are you a member of any associations? E.g. SNU, G.W.A. etc?
Billy answers: I have never trained with any such organizations as the SNU, The Spiritualist National Union, although I was a member of both

the SNU and the G.W.A - The Greater World Association. The reason I have not been trained by any such bodies is because I have never felt confident with their training programmes. I do not believe that they have the monopoly upon mediumship, and many of their so-called teachers are not qualified sufficiently to teach and train other mediums. This was the very reason I founded The Thought Workshop, and which was why it met great opposition from the SNU at the time.

The Clairvoyant questions The Parapsychologist - Billy asks Ciarán

As a parapsychologist, are you trying to disprove the existence of psychic skills, or trying to find out who genuinely possesses them?
Ciarán answers: I am fundamentally a scientist. For that reason I assess claims of psychic ability on a case-by-case basis. In providing sceptical explanations for psychic ability, I'm not out to disprove the existence of such skills, merely to provide sceptical knowledge to members of the public who may be faced with psychics in their daily lives. Give them the building blocks of knowledge to let them decide.

Do you accept that genuine mediums exist? If you don't, what do you suppose happens when we die, if anything?
Ciarán answers: There are two questions here. The first one regarding whether genuine mediums exist - yes, I've met mediums who genuinely believe they have ability; they are not frauds and, for the most part, are not utilizing cold reading methods. When subjected to scientific testing, however, they do not achieve positive results. The second question refers to my thoughts on what happens when we die - simple answer, I don't know. It is simply a matter of faith or belief to assume otherwise. We will all know the answer for sure when we die.

Can you tell us what you think happens when someone has an out-of-body experience?
Ciarán answers: Tough question since I've never had an OBE. But, from a psychological point of view, there is a lot of research on both sides of the camp (i.e. believer and cynic) that points towards a particular personality type that has OBEs. Such a person is highly suggestible, poorer at distinguishing reality from fantasy than non-OBE-ers, more likely to remember dreams from a bird's-eye perspective etc. So, some aspect of a particular person's personality means they are more likely to become deeply absorbed easily and this, combined with

possible neurological causes may constitute an OBE.

What do you think a ghostly apparition is?

Ciarán answers: A number of possible explanations exist for an eyewitness account of an apparition. These can be psychological or environmental or a combination of both. Psychological reasons can include suggestion (more powerful than you may think!), hypnogogic/hypnopompic hallucinations etc. Environmental can include temporal lobe epilepsy for example. There is a whole list of possible explanations that you have to discount first before you can go for a paranormal one. If you favour a paranormal one, there are many theories as to what an apparition actually is - stone-tape theory, water-memory theory etc. I think it's a good topic point you raise that we should cover later in the book.

Do you think that poltergeists are 'mischievous spirits' as defined in the dictionary, or do you believe there is a more scientific or logical reason for this phenomenon?

Ciarán answers: A lot of recent research on environmental causes of poltergeists has pointed to the possibility of local geomagnetic fields either creating a hallucinatory effect, or even physically causing the movement of objects. This is a relatively new area of research, but an exciting one and one that moves us ever closer to understanding the phenomena. A more logical reason concerns the mischievous and playful nature of the person the poltergeist activity is centred around. It is frequently an adolescent girl.

Do you believe in life after death, and if so where do you suppose this Spirit World is exactly?

Ciarán answers: Though I was brought up a Roman Catholic, I've since rejected religion and veered away from Faith generally. For this reason I remain agnostic about the idea of life after death and maybe this is a bi-product of my scientific mind. It doesn't prevent me for searching for evidence though, which may convince me otherwise.

Physicist, Oliver Lodge, devoted a lot of his life endeavouring to scientifically prove the existence of a Spirit World. 1) Do you suppose he would have shown such an interest had he not suffered the loss of his son, Raymond? In which case Lodge was just like everyone else who visits mediums, showing a great emotional need? 2) Do you know of any scientific breakthrough through where the Spirit World is concerned? If not will it ever happen, do you think?

Ciarán answers: You make a valid point about the emotional state of those who visit mediums. This makes them particularly vulnerable to messages that are given. Perhaps the same did occur with Sir Oliver Lodge. I like to think, however, that given his truly scientifically inquiring mind, he would have shown an active interest anyway and approached the subject with the fervour he did.

Scientific breakthroughs? It is an interesting question because any of the scientific evidence for mediumship would only prove evidence of paranormal communication (i.e. telepathy or mediumship) not any information about the Spirit World, or even evidence of its existence. Mediums have said to me in the past that they have provided accurate information to someone whilst working on the Spiritualist Church platform. The information is previously unknown to the medium and unknown to the person receiving the message. This is put forward as evidence of contact with the Spirit World. Not so, there are many other parapsychological processes that could be in play.

In your opinion do you think it is emotionally damaging to visit mediums on a regular basis?

Ciarán answers: I think an emotionally vulnerable population who visit mediums are prey to the sort of psychological damage that could harm someone who hasn't learnt to deal with grief. My view echoes that of other sceptics. There is no evidence, however, that this is the case. It is only speculation and true sceptics should remain open-minded to the possibility that visiting mediums may be beneficial until they see evidence countering that idea. That said, however, there is a greater possibility that visiting a medium is damaging the grieving process, but not only that, as a scientist I'm searching for the truth, how damaging is it for a grieving mother to receive a message from her departed son when the message is delivered by a fraudulent medium? How damaging is it for parents to receive a message that their son is dead only to find out years later that he had been abducted and is very much alive?

Do you think it is right for the church to decry mediums?
Ciarán answers: No. Aren't particular aspects of the church essentially mimicking the processes involved in mediumship? This is solely my opinion, however, since it's not my place to dictate what churches and religions should and shouldn't do.

Why do you think the church condemns mediums so harshly?
Ciarán answers: Perhaps because of the misinformed, but oft held association that mediumship has had with the occult. The word 'occult' is misconstrued as being a collective term for black magic and the dark arts and I think that's where the confusion and animosity may lie.

A high percentage of male mediums are gay. Why is this do you think?
Ciarán answers: Absolutely no idea. I would like to see cold hard stats on this idea before I pass further comment since it may be just your opinion. It may, however, have something to do with the idea that female intuition actually exists and that gay men are more in tune with their feminine side than heterosexual males, pure speculation. Saying this, I have a database of approx. 100 mediums and the majority are female.

Why do you think there are so many mediums today? Why are we humans so fascinated with the unknown and, in particular, the supernatural?
Ciarán answers: Perhaps people are becoming increasingly

disenchanted with science and the lack of answers that it has for all of their questions. Perhaps people are becoming increasingly disenchanted with religion and its constant stagnation in response to cultural changes. Perhaps the popularity of the paranormal in the media (TV, magazines, newspapers) and in other avenues such as ghost hunting, theatre shows etc., has provided easy money making opportunities for unscrupulous 'mediums'. Con artists have realized how easy it is to make a quick buck from people's grief. Perhaps mediumship is providing the answer for the majority of people. If they can't get the spiritual connection in a religious environment, perhaps they are attracted to a situation where they are solely responsible for their own religion, their own evidence.

There have been reports recently that scientists have discovered the module in the brain in which God exists. A paper has also been published showing a significant connection between frontal lobe epilepsy and religious experiences. As a parapsychologist, what is your opinion of this?
Ciarán answers: I think you mean temporal lobe epilepsy. As a parapsychologist one of things we attempt to do is discount every normal explanation for phenomena before we reach for a paranormal one. These neurological bases for experiences tie in with the general advancement in neuropsychology in general. Increasingly we are becoming aware of what the neurological basis is to a lot of psychological functions. I'm willing to accept it as an explanation if, as in science, the experiments are replicable, repeatable and conducted in a number of different labs.

Cats and dogs have an extremely accurate navigational system in their brains. They are able to navigate their route home by the position of the sun in the sky. Do you think that this ability is peculiar to animals only, or do you think the human psyche is capable of such things?
Ciarán answers: I'm not aware of this fact so difficult to comment

on cats and dogs but with regards to the human brain I think it could be possible. Read some of the anecdotal accounts given by anthropologists who observe aboriginals in their natural environment and it doesn't seem like such a leap. Interesting that you use 'brain' and 'psyche' in the same question. Does this mean you are a monist rather than a dualist?!

Psychometry literally means to 'measure with the mind'. I was always taught that it is not a mediumistic skill but a psychic one. Do you accept that psychometry works? If so, can you explain how it works?

Ciarán answers: No. I don't accept that there is paranormal evidence of it working. Certainly in uncontrolled situations psychics are able to come up with seemingly accurate items of information about the owner of an object but this occurs because of issues with language and cold reading techniques, not because of 'measuring with the mind'. In terms of it being a viable process, I think it's analogous to the claim of shaking someone's hand and being able to divine information about them, either telepathically or precognitively. For that reason, I'm open to the possibility of the process working, it's just that experimentally it's a nightmare to test and certainly there's no evidence of it actually working under those conditions.

If mediumship does not exist how did the phenomenon begin and why?

Ciarán answers: Many people refer back to 1848 and the Fox Sisters as the foundation of mediumship. This is incorrect. Certainly the Fox Sisters are credited with being the founders of Spiritualism as we know it, but the process of mediumship existed centuries before. For example, there are references to mediums in the Bible (e.g. I Samuel 28), the Witchcraft Act of 1735 actually covered communication with the dead, in 1744 Emanuel Swedenborg claimed he was in contact with the Spirit World, in 1844 Andrew Jackson Davies taught about the body's supernatural powers. Even before these historical references we find mention in some ancient Greek texts. So, perhaps we're looking at phenomena that exist as an instinctively human action. The great Scottish philosopher, Hume, thought so when he said that the mysterious and the supernatural can never truly be freed from human nature.

How would the human mind be affected if science proved, beyond a shadow of doubt, that there was absolutely nothing beyond death? Could we cope do you think?
Ciarán answers: Belief in various religions is defined as Faith. Faith is belief without evidence. There is such dogmatic faith in today's society that I don't think religion would be affected, I think followers would still follow and counter any scientific claims with 'evidential' claims made in their religion's writings (e.g. Bible). One needs only examine the ongoing argument between creationists and evolutionists to see how such an argument might develop. For those that are not so dogmatic, and given that the scientific evidence would have to be indisputable, it could create an element of anarchy. Sub-sections of the population would realize there are no consequences for their actions here on earth; they would realize we only have one life.

In your opinion is religion necessary?
Ciarán answers: It is necessary for some people, yes. For others, no.

In Victorian times Remote Viewing was called 'Distance Clairvoyance'. Can you explain what happens with this process?
Ciarán answers: It is defined by dictionaries as "The ability to perceive people, places, events, and objects by directing the consciousness to any destination provided via specified coordinates. There is no limit as to whether it's current or past, large or small, near or far." Interestingly, as you correctly point out, the process did actually exist in the past but perhaps there has been a term change to reflect a more scientific approach to the ability. This has been helped in no small part by the CIA's Stargate program, which examined the

possibility of using and training Remote Viewers for spy situations. The entire programme's results are available for public consumption, and although they make for long and hard reading, the overall finding is a positive one. There is an ongoing dialogue between Stargate researchers and others about possible explanations for the positive results and criticisms.

Instead of all the experiments you do on mediums and psychics, wouldn't it be easier and far more effective to use a polygraph (lie detector)? Or do you think that some alleged psychics are so self-deluded that they would defy such apparatus?

Ciarán answers: My other area of research is Investigative Psychology that is a behavioural science approach to criminal investigations which looks at cognitive processes and social psychological theory. This particular specialized area of criminal psychology takes a critical look at many claims made by advisors external to criminal investigations. One of those claims is the use of polygraph, and certainly its admittance in a court of law (the norm in US courts, inadmissible in the UK). The results are inconclusive, meaning there is research on both sides of the camps - it works, it doesn't. The only consistent results are obtained with the style of questioning. For example, if the suspect under examination is accused of stealing £500, the questions, once he's hooked up to a polygraph, would be ...

a. Did you steal £150?
b. Did you steal £500?
c. Did you steal £400?

Only the guilty would respond to the correct amount. The difficultly is trying to find a comparable line of questioning for mediums. Additionally, researchers know that state of mind plays a huge effect (i.e. stress) and produces inaccurate results. You also raise a good point - an honest answer on a polygraph would not necessarily always be a genuinely honest answer, you may get someone severely deluded so they 'fool' the polygraph.

Chapter 5
Ghosts & Things that go 'Bump' in the Night!

The Parapsychologist - Ciarán O'Keeffe

Hauntings

Haunting phenomena, including poltergeist-like episodes, has been defined as visual, auditory, and olfactory experiences; sensed presence, including the feeling of not being alone, or a touch; erratic functioning of equipment, usually of a mechanical or electrical nature; unexplained strong emotional episodes; and object movement. Haunting phenomena has also been described as "anomalous sensory experiences and physical changes in the environment".

There is now an accumulating body of evidence, and theories, alleging that known conventional physical energies may be mediating or allegedly causing hauntings and poltergeist-like episodes. These energies include *ionizing radiation, geomagnetic activity, infrasonic sound waves and localized electromagnetic and electrostatic fields.* Certain researchers have said that extreme or unusual forms of electromagnetic fields (EMFs) can directly influence the physical environment and the psychophysiological functioning of those who are exposed.

There are many different methods for investigating haunted locations. Haunting phenomena have traditionally been researched through observational and quite personal, experience-focused methods. This would frequently entail entering a haunted location and attempting to have the same occurrence experienced by previous eyewitnesses. The first research that attempted to assess, in a more scientific way, the personal (subjective) experiences, occurred about 40 years ago. This work was the first to approach subjective reports through the use of quantitative statistical analyses of adjective checklists and floor plans. The approach has subsequently been improved by other researchers. It should be pointed out, however, that the majority of this work is limited to the analysis of subjective reports and not objective measurement. Given the sceptical explanations discussed previously, I recommend that observational and survey methods are used along with specialized monitoring equipment capable of detecting small variations of the environment.

There is a prevalence of evidence of haunting phenomena, which includes physical examples such as a photograph or film and personal ones such as feeling a presence, or sensing a drop in temperature. For this evidence to stand up against scientific scrutiny an investigator needs to have discounted all possible alternative explanations. For example, a witness who reports a sense of presence in a haunted location could be experiencing naturally occurring infrasound, they may have been affected by temporal lobe epilepsy, they may be interpreting a quite natural drop in temperature as the presence of a spirit, they may be prone to the suggestion that the location is haunted and, as a result, their mind 'runs riot' (to put it scientifically!). It is important, therefore, to accumulate as much information as possible to make the evidence count.

Poltergeist

Poltergeist phenomena are commonly defined, in Parapsychology, as "displays of energy that induce movement of objects which are ordinarily held in place by inertia and gravity". It is a word derived from German, meaning, literally, 'noisy spirit' (poltern - noisy, geist - spirit) and phenomena can also include loud noises, the appearance of water, apports and asports, and even spontaneous fires. Parapsychologists also refer to poltergeist as recurrent spontaneous psychokinesis or RSPK. The reason for this is recognition of potential causes of the phenomena as being more to do with living people in a location rather than spirits. William Roll, the parapsychologist most well-known for researching poltergeist cases, feels that poltergeist events reflect psychological tension between a central person involved in the case and others, including, perhaps, investigators. In addition, poltergeist phenomena typically occur for a limited period of time (e.g. the Enfield

Poltergeist happened for approximately 18 months) as opposed to hauntings which can last for centuries.

The idea that poltergeist activity is centred solely around a young girl, often a teenager, has been aided, in no small part, due to a popular film from 1982. In this film a family are plagued by the movement of household objects (e.g. kitchen chairs) and apparitions, before being confronted with an apparent door 'to the other side'. The implication is that the activity is focused around Carol Anne, the youngest daughter in the family. Though there is a commonly held belief that pubescent girls are the catalyst for such events, the origin for it comes from late nineteenth century psychical researchers. Households in the late nineteenth century would have been comprised of large families with children undoubtedly being members. It is no surprise also that when rowdy, undetermined disturbances such as banging and flying objects occurred, the clear culprits would be youngsters with uncontrollable energy and prankish tendencies. Indeed, poltergeist research is plagued by the discovery of fraud and trickery.

The most famous example of this controversy surrounding poltergeist occurred in March 1983. Tina Resch, aged 14, had been the centre of disturbances in her home in Columbus, Ohio. Activity included the regular movement of small household objects and larger objects (e.g. mattresses, dressers etc). The phenomena were also recorded in a lab (the Spring Creek Institute in the US) by Dr. Baumann and William Roll. They had brought Tina into the lab with the intention of replicating the phenomena. She was hypnotized in order to evoke the bodily sensations associated with the events in her home. Objects used as targets included a 12 inch socket wrench which moved 18 feet passed the two experimenters and Tina. All in all there were 21 movements of objects when Tina was under observation, of which eight came from a specially prepared 'target' table. In addition to this compelling evidence from the lab, Roll had also investigated the case at Tina's home in the previous year and declared it to be authentic. Reports were given of 'flying' telephones, swinging lamps and a multitude of loud noises. The controversy surrounding this case comes from the media interest. In one incident a camera from a TV crew was inadvertently left running and captured Tina cheating by pulling over a lamp whilst unobserved. Also, investigation of the case by the contentious figure, James Randi, showed that the majority of occurrences were press inventions or highly exaggerated descriptions of natural events. The case has a tragic end; Tina Resch was propelled into a downward spiral that led to an abusive marriage, a divorce, and the birth of a child -- all before her twentieth birthday. Three years later she was charged with that child's murder, and she is currently serving a life sentence for a crime as controversial, mysterious, and complex as the accused herself -- a crime she maintains she did not commit. Poltergeists, for me, are the most fascinating aspect of investigations and certainly the most compelling for people to hear about or watch on TV, but they are also the most frustrating. Let me explain why.

First, I want to add to the previous definition given by talking a little more about the multitude of exciting phenomena poltergeists are said to produce. As well as the usual "raps, taps, thumps, thuds, crashes, bangs and bombinations", poetically phrased by the renowned investigator/researcher Alan Gauld, there could be the movement of objects, musical instruments playing, fires, the deluge of water, interference with electrical equipment (e.g. radios, TVs, light bulbs etc), clothes tearing…the list continues. It's rare to find a case where all this phenomena occurs. Indeed, many of you may have experienced simple taps or thumps (check the water pipes!), or the movement of objects (try and capture it on film!) but to have experienced everything from paranormal arson to clothing vandalism would be truly out-of-this-world!

The Miami Poltergeist of 1966-67 springs to mind when I'm questioned about 'extreme' cases where lots of different phenomena occur. Over 224 separate incidents were recorded over a period of several months, all centred around a 19-year-old named Julio Vasquez. Over 120 happened whilst two well-known parapsychologists were investigating (Dr. Roll and Dr. Pratt). What is more remarkable is that

44 incidents happened whilst one or other of them was actually watching. The investigators set up a test for macro-PK by using drinking glasses and other objects as targets and placing them in the active areas. Ten of the targets moved when no one was near, including Julio, the 19-year-old agent.

Another great case is the Olive Hill Case. Roger, the grandson of John and Ora Callihan was said, again by Dr. Roll, to be the RSPK, or poltergeist, agent. I'll leave it to Dr. Roll to describe some of the most impressive phenomena (approx. 180 incidents occurred):

"...When I was standing in the doorway between the living room and the children's bedroom, I saw a bottle fly off the dresser and land four feet away. It did not slide off and roll into the room but was clearly airborne. When this took place, Roger was in my peripheral vision on my right in the living room, walking away. His sister was standing slightly behind me on my left; there was no one else in the room. I could discover no way in which the event could have been faked. At one point, I was following Roger into the kitchen, when the kitchen table flew up, rotated 45 degrees and fell down on the backs of the chairs that stood around it, its four legs off the floor. Roger and the table were in full view when this happened."

With such amazing, compelling and verified cases, why is it 'frustrating' as I indicated earlier? The main reason is that the majority of evidence comes from eyewitness accounts and researchers who have been unable to put in the appropriate controls to prevent fraud. In the same way that magicians should be consulted when examining claims of psychic/mediumship ability, they should also be consulted for poltergeist claims. You'd understand my concern if you ever had the opportunity to see great magicians perform tricks of levitating objects, electrical disturbances or spontaneous fires. It's then that you realize that only when a poltergeist case is investigated and the phenomena captured on film and the possibility of magic, or fraud, or an environmental cause (e.g. open window!), has been prevented could you then say it must be paranormal.

In addition to the ones highlighted above I've listed a few more cases that fascinate me. In my previous book *Ghosthunters*, I wrote about the Enfield Poltergeist, so I won't repeat myself here, but I encourage anyone who hasn't heard about it to find accounts now. It's extremely compelling. The additional fascinating cases I've described below have been chosen for their uniqueness. Poltergeist phenomena have traditionally been a topic of study through observation and survey methods. It should be pointed out that the cases presented below are based on subjective reports and not objective measurement.

Cases that fascinate me
The Phelps Case

The Reverend Dr. Eliakim Phelps, his wife and four children (girls aged 16 and 6, boys aged 11 and 3) lived in Stratford, Conneticut. Rev. Phelps, days before the poltergeist disturbances began, held a séance and received replies to his questions in the form of rapping noises. The disturbances actually occurred between March 1850 and October 1851. The first indication of activity was when the family returned from church to find the entire house ransacked and a 'corpse' made of clothing laid out in the middle of the floor. Following this, objects moved about in front of various witnesses (including individual members of the family and neighbours). Small items such as cutlery, keys and nails were thrown about. Furniture apparently moved of its own accord in front of witnesses, and also was rearranged when family members had left a particular room. They reported the unusual sensation of the house literally 'shaking'. In one of the rooms the family found clothing and cushions had been used to form 11 life-sized figures (10 female). They were displayed in devotional poses with bibles open in front of them. Centrally placed was a dwarf-like figure, and a final figure was suspended 'as though flying through the air'.

On one occasion when the Reverend had turned away from his writing desk to leave the room he heard a scratching sound (i.e. writing). He turned back to find 'Very nice paper and nice ink for the devil' written on the paper on the desk. The elder boy experienced levitation. He was seen to be "carried across the room by invisible hands and gently deposited on the floor". The boy also woke twice to find himself outside, as if he'd been carried in his sleep. The elder girl was hit, her pillow pushed in her face and her neck tied up with tape. Strangest of all, a "vegetable growth sprouted out of the carpet before the eyes of the family". The leaves were said to be covered with strange hieroglyphics.

One of the few primary accounts has Phelps reporting in an interview, the following:

The phenomena have been entirely unexplicable (sic) to me. I have followed the slow movement of objects through the air, observing carefully their direction, their slow movement, and their curving flight, and am convinced that they were not moved by any human agency... the noises are most violent when all the family are present, especially when they were seated at the table... I place no value in any of the messages, and if they are from spirits they are from evil spirits. I am satisfied that the communications are wholly worthless, and that they are frequently false, contradictory and nonsensical; the spirits often accuse each other of lying and constantly inflicting injury on persons and property... fifty-six articles were picked up at one time which had been thrown at someone's head. Thirty figures were seen, and twenty window panes broken... The phenomena for the past several weeks have been subsiding, and have now ceased entirely, I hope!

The Parker Case

In the mid-1950s, in the USA, Jim and Susan Parker were affected by a variety of highly unusual poltergeist phenomena. Aside from hearing a loud voice, they were witness to dirt literally being 'tipped' into their caravan where they were living at the time. Additionally a bed became soaked with the contents of a cesspit. Following repeatable phenomenon of the sort already described (including traditional feelings of unease), Susan and Jim witnessed blood pouring through the join between the wall and the ceiling in the caravan's living room. The amount of blood was estimated to be about ten gallons and, following laboratory examination, was found to be pig's blood.

Spirit Lights, Orbs or What?

On a daily basis I'm presented with photographic evidence of ghosts. At least, that's what the email says. More often than not, the attached photo shows an 'orb', the supposed first manifestation of spirit. I don't buy it. The revolution in digital imaging and photography in general has brought with it an increase in reports of spirit lights. It's essentially all to do with the development of digital photography. As well as possible capturing of reflections from minute objects such as dust, insects, water droplets, even breath particles, there is the issue of the digital cameras filling in the blanks. The highly regarded investigative group, Para.Science, has conducted extensive research on the topic. This excerpt from their website sums it up perfectly.

> *A 3 megapixel CCD (i.e. digital camera) actually captures less than 10% of the total image information available within a scene when compared with a 35mm camera negative. The software has to 'fill in' these gaps in the image by making comparisons with the information from neighbouring pixels, thus a single pin point of light in a scene may be ignored completely or seen and then 'expanded' by the software as it compares and interpolates each pixel with it's neighbours- the single point source of light becoming a gradually larger and fainter circle of light - giving the characteristic circular Orb anomaly. The CCD also had a further trick to play - sometimes individual photodiodes may not respond correctly to the light falling on them sending a signal that is either 100% on or 100% off - again, the software would 'expand' these white specs into circular Orbs - Black Orbs, caused by the 100% 'off state' are also possible and are seen, but only rarely as they tend to blend into the background of the image more quickly.*
>
> *- www.parascience.org.uk*

The Clairvoyant - Billy Roberts
Corner of the Eye

An extremely high percentage of psychic apparitions occur in the peripheral vision and usually disappear when the eyes are moved to focus directly on them. This phenomenon is referred to as the 'corner of the eye syndrome' and is extremely common. I experienced this frequently during my sojourn into the world of music, particularly when I was playing my guitar. Although I nearly always managed to ignore them, there were the odd occasions when they just would not be ignored. I became quite used to the distraction of dancing figures of light in my peripheral vision, and would often watch them, enthralled by their visual display. I soon learnt that there was little use in trying to eliminate them from my sight, and that 'they' were determined to remain with me forever.

Spirit Lights

Ever since I can remember, Spirit Lights have been an integral part of my life in one way or another. What is seen today on television are not Spirit Lights or 'orbs' as it is fashionable to call them. Spirit Lights are usually focuses of intense light and are usually, but not always, an indication that there is a discarnate presence. Although they often do move around the room, they very rarely move in a straight horizontal line across one's vision, as they are often seen on certain television programmes. When a room is in total darkness, Spirit Lights often appear in the corner of a room and once one's attention is caught by them, they sometimes gyrate in front of you, almost in attempt to entertain you. Over the years I have learnt that the colours of Spirit Lights can vary, from intense white light to blue and even red. The colour is often an indication of whom they represent, either in relation to your family, or perhaps in relation to Spirit Guides etc. Some Spirit Lights are no more than concentrations of energy and may not be Spirits at all. These sorts of Spirit Lights occur when energy collects to form an objective luminous vortex, which can be seen by anyone who happens to be present at the time. They can also be the product of other more scientific phenomena, such as Triboluminescence, the phenomena caused by the friction of two pieces of quartz or other geological materials. Ionized air may be another causal factor of so-called Spirit Lights. So I think it would be silly to attribute all light manifestations to spirits, when there could be other more logical causes.

As a child I used to lie in bed watching Spirit Lights dancing round my room, usually in the farthest corner, high up against the ceiling. I suppose it was more effective than counting sheep, as they always lulled me to sleep within minutes.

The phenomenon of Triboluminescence

Some scientific research has concluded that, not only do we humans have a Bioplasmic body, made up of minute particles of energy with a self-created light, but that also the universe itself is filled with Bioplasmic energy upon which is recorded every moment of human experience. It is some researcher's theory that this Bioplasmic energy is perhaps the memory itself of the planet upon which we live, and that we occasionally experience this memory when we 'see' apparitions, phantoms or ghosts, whatever you choose to call them. This then would suggest that not all apparitions are the spirit manifestations of the so-called dead, and so, therefore, we are merely watching a replay of past events and people long-since gone. Although still within the parameters of paranormal science, these visions, strictly speaking, are not 'ghosts'. Some people, because of an abnormality in the brain, seem to be able to 'tap into' this memory bank quite easily, and although we frequently refer to them as mediums, a more suitable definition would be 'memory sensitive'.

The same kinds of people are extremely sensitive to Triboluminescence, the geological phenomenon produced by the friction of quartz deposits or other mineral substances below ground. This phenomenon produces changes in the electro-magnetic atmosphere, and causes an interruption in the electrical circuitry in the brains of certain individuals in the location. All this electro-magnetic 'chaos' causes some people to experience a 'psychic overload', the effects of which are just like imbibing a hallucinogenic substance. If the individual remains within the confines of the phenomena produced by the Triboluminescence, they will have all sorts of transcendental experiences, very similar to seeing things clairvoyantly. However, this phenomenon only accounts for a minority of paranormal activity; the majority may be attributed to spirit or metaphysical phenomena. As I have previously stated, over the past few years I have become very critical of the whole subject matter and have begun making a detailed analysis of the different kinds of mediums and paranormal phenomena. Although I have been mediumistically inclined since I was a child, I am going to have to reserve my judgement about the whole concept of mediumship and the paranormal, at least until the conclusion of this book.

The Haunted House Syndrome

I have been exploring paranormal locations for over twenty five years, but with the growing popularity of *Most Haunted* and other similar paranormal television programmes today, the whole subject has gone ridiculously crazy. From such programmes new terminology has evolved, and it would seem that everyone who watches these programmes has become an 'expert' on the subject. I am wondering whether more damage has been done by television, and whether the paranormal is today viewed with a less serious eye than it was perhaps ten years ago. In fact, in my experience I have found only an extremely small portion of paranormal disturbances in houses to actually be the products of discarnate spirits. In the majority of so-called 'Haunted' locations the cause of paranormal activity can very often be located at a geological level. In fact, it has been found that geological disturbances below ground can affect significant changes in the magnetic field in the surrounding area, thus affecting the right temporal lobe in the brains of certain susceptible people. This can result in hallucinations, and can even allow certain people to mentally connect with a subtle memory bank. Although the person may experience a 'hallucination', as a consequence of the fluctuations in the magnetic field, the hallucinations are primarily the product of the image-making faculty of the brain. Whilst the person is living in this electro-magnetically disturbed environment, he or she will have 'psychic' experiences, and may either 'see' or 'hear' echoes from the past. Once the person moves away these so-called psychic experiences usually cease, but not always.

When a person has been told they are going to a haunted location, their mind creates the ghosts and demons long before they reach their destination. The whole psychology of the subject is debatable and open to ridicule. In fact, it is very difficult for anyone with a serious interest in the paranormal to remain rational and calm when investigating paranormal activity. There seems to be a certain kind of hysteria, peculiar to the paranormal investigator that somehow prevents any object conclusions as to the true nature of a haunting. When I watch paranormal television programmes, I can see how fire of this mad craze is fuelled. The whole subject has gone crazy, and this is the real reason why it attracts so much distain and cynicism.

Chapter 6
Perceptions of the Spirit World

The Clairvoyant - Billy Roberts

Whilst all mediums are different and therefore work in different ways, their aims should be the same, to prove that the soul survives death to live on in a different sphere. I am quite certain that it is the concept of a Spirit World that the majority of people have difficulty accepting.

The misconception most people have is that the Spirit World is a place; a place that is invisible to us mortals. This notion is completely wrong as the Spirit World has nothing whatsoever to do with places; it is a condition or transcendental state of being. Although it has no particular geographical place in the universe, it could be said that the Spirit World lies in all places, because technically, it permeates the entire universe. It is an axiom of physics that no two bodies of matter can exist in the same space at the same time. However, millions upon millions of vibrations can exist in the same place at the same time, without in anyway interfering with each other. We live in a multidimensional universe in which there are worlds within worlds, each rising in a gradually ascending vibratory scale, from the very lowest of the physical world, to the very highest Spiritual realms. In fact, the Spirit World orbits within and around the physical atom and interpenetrates the physical world. Those who inhabit the Spirit World live and walk through us, completely unaware of our presence, just as we are unaware of theirs. In other words, we are invisible to them, just as they are invisible to us. However, whilst our physical world is solid and substantial to us, the Spirit World is solid and substantial to those who live in it. There are no alternating periods of night and day, and in the Spirit World there is a continual process of learning and spiritually evolving. This does not mean that the debauched and the villain become angelic beings as soon as they make the transition into the Spirit World; on the contrary. The less spiritually minded souls have to remain in the lower vibratory planes of existence, until such time that their consciousness has sufficiently evolved and they are ready to leave behind the instinctive natures of their lower selves. Only then will they be allowed to gain access to the higher vibratory planes of existence.

A medium is simply a person whose mind is able to 'home in' to the varying vibratory states of the Spirit World, and can either sense, see or hear its inhabitants. In other words, he or she possesses an in-built antenna to receive impulses from the super-sensual side of the universe.

The Parapsychologist - Ciarán O'Keeffe

I have a real problem with reported concepts of the Spirit World. In my opinion there are a number of issues regarding the evidence about a Spirit World. We're reliant on a number of different debatable sources for this evidence - Near Death Experiences (NDEs), religion, communication from Spirit and the perceptions of mediums. NDEs are a controversial area and have been studied extensively since Raymond Moody first published his book, *Life after Life*, in 1975. There are arguments on both sides of the debate regarding whether the accounts from people who have had NDEs are a true representation of the journey to the Spirit World. Convincing explanations have been put forward by anaesthetists and neurologists, as well as some parapsychologists, regarding the imagery such an experient witnesses, and how the neurology of the brain shutting down can explain it. Additionally the experiences are only an indication of the 'journey' *towards* the hereafter. Typical imagery involves tunnels, bright lights etc, but witness descriptions of the actual Spirit World never happen because the person is brought back from the brink of death before they reach that world.

The wealth of evidence, therefore, comes from religion, Spirit and the perceptions of mediums. Out there, somewhere, there may be a medium that *is* getting genuine messages from a departed spirit describing the Spirit World. There may be one religion, above all others, whose concept of heaven is the right one. There may be a medium that, through trance, relays wondrous descriptions of Spirit World around them. There may be an apparition that has interacted with a living person and given details about life after death. There may be, but in the words of the Committee for Skeptical Inquiry, "I doubt it!"

The reason I express this doubt is because the multitude of descriptions relayed from the Spirit World seem to be inconsistent or so vague and ambiguous one wonders whether it's worth getting the descriptions at all. Sylvia Browne describes a "higher-frequency dimension" where the "colors are brighter, and the flowers are more gorgeous and far larger than on your plane," and James Van Praagh has a similar concept of heaven as a world "very much like our physical world with similar sights and sounds, although more vivid and colourful". Sorry, I should clarify, it wasn't Sylvia Browne who gave that description it was Francine, a spirit channelled by Sylvia. There are frequently references to the ancient belief that 'heaven' has many levels. For example, Mia Dolan (from her guide, Eric) discusses the idea that we are a higher self and a lower self and that while on Earth "only your lower self is awake" and there isn't strictly a hell but our higher self judges which level we go to.

We frequently hear a sort of 'get out clause' from mediums regarding the Spirit World. By this I mean the sort of descriptions where inconsistency, or differences between spirits, is explained. A good example would be Gordon Smith's opinion "that we create our own kingdom come, that each individual arrives at a place where they will find comfort and beauty according to the state of their own mind when departing from this world". In addition, look through other texts and you'll find yet more afterlife concepts: Arbatel's 'Seven Stewards of Heaven'; Andrew Jackson Davis' Summerland; Swedenborg's communications with Angels from the Spirit World who only communicate in vowels; Chinese Confucian belief in Tian; the Polynesian Tuamotus concept of the universe and 'left and right' heavens (nine of them); Borri's luminous palm branch reserved for him in heaven; the narrow, thread-like, bridge called the 'brig of dead' which one has to cross to enter heaven, etc. This is besides the competing concepts of the afterlife found in 'mainstream' religions (e.g. Roman Catholicism, Islam, Judaism, Church of Jesus Christ of Latter-Day Saints etc). Am I being a bit harsh and perhaps arrogant? Who am I to say which concept of the Spirit World is the right one? Quite right, but then I haven't said which one is right, I'm just a bit confused.

Chapter 7
The Truth about Mediums?

The Parapsychologist - Ciarán O'Keeffe
I'm only saying these things just in case, you see. I don't know what's coming...Farmhouse, very country conditions...Woman in the house, dark hair. Left side, left side...Pathology department, studying bones, hand. Skeleton...of hand, white coats. Investigation, bone. Unsolved. Mystery...Man with no name. Norman. Flat, high above shop...
- Excerpt from an anonymous 'psychic detective's' account of a double homicide.

Psychic Criminology
'Psychic Criminology' is a misleading term that refers to any involvement of the paranormal in criminal investigations (not just psychic involvement). This can take the form of psychics using psychometry on a murder weapon, to dowsing on a map to divine the location of a missing person, to the more common involvement of a medium attempting to communicate with a murder victim to get details of the murderer. It has captured our imagination for centuries. From Jacques Aymar's use of dowsing in locating the murderer of a wine-grower and his wife in 1692, to over 300 years later and a family's request to employ a medium in the police-led search for their missing daughter. Despite numerous studies highlighting the poor performance of supposed psychic detectives, and the abundant anecdotal reports of embarrassing failures, there is still a tendency for psychics and mediums to be considered viable by some in criminal investigations. If the ability was reliable wouldn't it be put to better use lowering the crime rate by solving burglaries, theft, fraud, robbery and rape? In the grand scheme of things, murders account for a small percentage of crimes committed in the UK and unsolved murders a smaller percentage still. It's no surprise, however, that high profile unsolved

murders or child abduction cases bring psychics and mediums out in droves. On the one hand, the media coverage of such cases evokes sympathy in genuine, though some would argue, misguided mediums and psychics and a willingness to help the bereaved parents or family members. On the other hand, the sensationalist nature of the case potentially provides the perfect platform for frauds wanting to achieve fame and recognition.

Some researchers believe that "hope and uncertainty evoke powerful psychological processes that keep all occult and pseudoscientific character readers in business". This may go some way to explaining their continued use, but little research has focused on why we hear testimonies from various police departments (specifically the US) as to a medium's success, when, following retrieval of the statements made, the information given appears to be little more than a collection of vagueness and ambiguity.

Studies suggest that psychics and mediums are no more accurate than anybody else in assessing characteristics of offenders from crime scene material. Despite this, a survey back in 1993 established that 35 per cent of urban United States police departments and 19 per cent of rural departments admit to having used a psychic at least once in their investigations. Authors of a fantastic book on the subject entitled *The Blue Sense* also report the widespread use of psychic detectives in Britain, Holland, Germany and France. There are, doubtless, a variety of reasons why such individuals are still employed, not least of which is the fact that police departments do have an obligation to take all information provided on a case seriously. They can never be sure whether the information is coming from an associate of the criminal or victim who wishes to remain anonymous or who doesn't want to reveal their source. As soon as a police officer records the information received it can then be described by a psychic detective as a situation where they "provided the police with information on a case and it was noted". The false impression then is that the psychic or medium assisted in the investigation.

One factor that may contribute to their widespread use, both in criminal investigations, and in other situations (e.g. face-to-face readings, theatres etc) is the extent to which they shun logic in favour of emotional appeal. In other words, where conventional deduction has failed, romantic drama and emotional involvement may succeed.

In the past in my experimental work with psychics and mediums in a simulated murder investigation scenario I've found that the mediums' statements sound more *confident* and *dramatic* than those produced by either students or forensic experts (e.g. psychologists or detectives). Some American researchers have also suggested that individuals might be persuaded more by the dramatic character of the mediums' information produced rather than by its objective merit. Although these speculations allude to how psychic detectives, and therefore psychics and mediums generally, may convince and persuade people to accept the accuracy of information, they do not go far in presenting an underlying substantive rationale as to *why* or *how* such accounts appear so convincing. I think it's because when we listen to a reading we become actively involved in making it right.

The Truth about Mediums?

Leaving aside accusations of fraud, my theory is that the majority of psychics and mediums rely heavily on *involving* the listener. Any words, or way of delivering a reading, that encourages active involvement will generate a more positive assessment. This is especially true of face-to-face readings but could also be the case, to a lesser extent, in churches or theatres. A particularly useful definition of *involvement* is:

An internal, even emotional connection individuals feel which binds them to other people as well as to places, things activities, ideas, memories and words... I see it as not a given but an achievement in conversational interaction
- Tannen (1996, p. 12)

This connects closely to a feeling of rapport between medium and client. The issue of promoting involvement also lies at the heart of successful cold reading which I've mentioned before:

> "once the client is actively engaged in trying to make sense of the series of sometimes contradictory statements issuing from the reader, he becomes a creative problem solver trying to find coherence and meaning in the total set of statements"
> - (Hyman, 1989)

Indeed, many of the linguistic devices discussed within the area of cold reading are merely ways to hook the client in and get them involved in what's being said. These devices are discussed below:

Fishing

People tend to accept vague and ambiguous personality descriptions as uniquely applicable to themselves without realizing that the same description could be applied to just about anyone (remember the Barnum Effect that I mentioned earlier?). Fishing consists of obtaining the information from the listener in order to feed it back later on in the reading. For example, a psychic may say, "I see the letter R." The client may indicate some reaction, a body or verbal cue, in which case the psychic will say, "Rob........or Roger," at which point the client may say, "It must be Rodney Jones!"

Base-rate information or high probability statements disguised to appear as though they are obtained through extraordinary means may also be employed. In a study in the 1950s two psychologists, highly experienced in interpreting the outcome of the MMPI, wrote a personality sketch for each student on the basis of his or her test results. Each student then received two personality sketches - the one actually written for him or her and one prepared by a psychologist prior to the study (a 'stock spiel'). When asked to pick which described him or her better, 26 of the 44 students picked the fake sketch. Part of the reason for this relies on the fact that the information in the profile could be applicable to anyone. Similarly, cold readers can use vague and ambiguous statements in order to rely on the interpretative framework of the listener to 'fill in the gaps'.

Other similar devices have been explored extensively and possibly this process of relying on the listener to fill in the gaps may be preferred for two reasons: Firstly, to save face if something the medium says is not well received, and secondly to achieve the sense of rapport that comes from being understood. The former relates to what stage magicians refer to as 'multiple outs' where, if the reading heads in one direction unsuccessfully, the reader can adjust the direction easily. The second relates to the necessary requirement of building rapport between the reader and the client.

Dramatisation and Imagery

An imaginative use of language can evoke particularly strong emotional responses in a listener. It's no surprise also that reporting speech as direct speech creates more vivid accounts. I believe that this is because reporting the 'present tense' of the speech stirs the imagination of the listener more readily. In the same way, the temporal and spatial features of readings are affected by tense (present, past or future) and locational words. By locational words I mean words like 'here', 'there', 'now' and 'then'. With particular locational words, though, the listener is 'located' more closely to the speaker or psychic. For example, the words 'here' and 'there' are closer, more present, more proximal, more engaging. It's a lot more exciting and engaging to hear a psychic detective say "I can feel the man's hands tighten around my neck here" compared to "He then strangled her." The use of the locational words and putting the action in the present make it more convincing.

I've also observed that changes in voice quality and intonation can mark specific utterances representing a different voice (think of alleged 'possessions' by certain self-professed mediums). Thus the use of direct speech and the voice mimicking leads to a more dynamic involvement of the listener. The use of direct speech appears to be very common in accounts given by psychics - particularly when the voice is that of the deceased.

Additionally, an important factor in the expression of mutual participation lies in the psychic's ability to create images that the listener will be able to identify with. Constructing images serves to set scenes, to provide a sense of authenticity and to contribute to the purpose of the story and to the presentation of self. I think there is great importance in the use of imagery and detail in conveying meaning and in arousing emotional qualities in the listener.

Staging modesty
Frequently psychics profess modesty about their talents. Even the most reputable psychics use this technique. Individuals consumed by self admiration can expect to win little admiration. Modesty and humility concerning one's qualifications is often more effective. The Israeli psychic, Uri Geller, for example, in a recorded experiment in New Zealand, stated, "...today, I'm not in the exact mood to do it, so it'll take longer..." and then proceeded to complete four apparent ESP feats in less than 20 minutes. This initial modesty then almost arouses a sense of sympathy in the client, they almost will the medium to do well, actively searching for confirmation of what the medium says, becoming...yes, you guessed it, more involved.

Co-operative strategies
I have read manuals in the pseudo-psychic and magic literature which recommends to potential 'psychics' that they should emphasize to the client that the success of the reading depends as much on the co-operation of the listener as on the psychic and that it is imperative that successful rapport is established.

Successful and co-operative discourse is a product of rhythmic and simultaneous discourse. For example, successful conversation could be set to a metronome and, anecdotally, counsellors have reported being able to derive more useful information from interviews when rhythm was established. There are several examples where arrhythmic asymmetry in discourse can relate to conversational 'disasters' in relationships and at work.

In keeping with the 'musical' analogy it has also been shown that recurrent patterns of repetition make for conversational rapport. For example, alliteration (use of same consonant, e.g. sinister stalker), self-repetition, allo-repetition (echoing of others) and rhyme all contribute to involvement between speaker and listener. Such patterns have long been a focus in the study of everyday conversation and are a reflection of the extent to which repetitive and almost ritualized expressions are common in talk.

I've noticed another language device that underpins this entire process: the attempt to empathize with a sceptical population prior to introducing the paranormal aspects of the account. To illustrate, the psychic testimonies of Noreen Reiner often commenced with the portrayal of a logical individual casting doubt on paranormal occurrences: "I used to be a sceptic and then one day a psychic did some stuff on me, then I started practising, trying to disprove this stuff existed." This process of identifying with the listener allows for subsequent presentation of the psychic's argument and is a process that has been recognized for centuries and is a direct reflection of the psychic's attempt to involve the audience.

The psychic/medium reading is therefore shaped in part by the demands of the interactive situation, the conversation (even if parts of it are non-verbal). I suggest that the demand placed on the psychic or medium is to involve the listener in interpreting the account and that this may go someway in explaining, from a psychological and linguistic point of view, why certain readings appear to be more accurate or impressive than they actually are and, more importantly why some clients give glowing reports of their interaction with a medium - especially when the testimonials do not match an actual reading of the medium's message. The interaction with a medium is a psychological minefield that works in the medium's favour. Additionally, and this is where I'll stop my sceptical rant, the *involvement* aspect of a reading continues beyond its conclusion. Days later the assessment of the reading's accuracy benefits from something called 'retro-fitting' or 'selective memory', where the client only remembers the hits or literally 'fills in the gaps' of a reading. Also there are the usual fallibility issues surrounding eyewitness testimony which we know from forensic psychology research. Essentially it is very difficult for anyone to remember with 100 per cent clarity or accuracy every word of a reading even the next day. Given everything that I've said in this section is it any wonder that mediumship readings may appear more accurate than they actually are?

The Clairvoyant - Billy Roberts

Having appeared on innumerable radio and television programmes with various parapsychologists over the years, I do understand exactly what Ciarán is saying about mediums and the way in which they work. The problem is that it is far easier to disprove mediumistic skills than it is to validate them. And yes, a lot of the information given by many mediums is very general and could apply to anyone. However, let's not discount the more specific information that could only apply to the person to whom the message is given. For example, a deceased person's first and second name and the name of the street where he or she lived. Combine this information with a detailed description and the names of others in the communicator's family, you then have fairly conclusive evidence that some sort of skill most certainly exists. Where does this information come from if not from a discarnate mind? One parapsychologist described such phenomena as 'mind reading'. He was willing to accept the phenomenon of mind reading but dismissed the possibility that a medium could receive information from a discarnate source. As a result of their training, most parapsychologists are more intent on disproving the whole mediumistic theory, and even when they experience extraordinary phenomena it still fails to break through his or her academic armour. I think what parapsychologists are actually saying is either that when you are dead you are dead, or that it is absolutely impossible for a corporeal mind to receive any communication whatsoever from an incorporeal mind. Whether or not such information given by a medium actually proves the survival of the human soul is perhaps another point for discussion. However, it does prove that the mind of a medium is somewhat different to that of a person with absolutely no mediumistic skills whatsoever. Parapsychology is the study of supposed mental phenomena that cannot be explained by known psychological or scientific principles, e.g. extrasensory perception and telepathy. The word 'Paranormal' very generally means, 'Impossible to explain scientifically. Unable to be explained or understood in terms of scientific knowledge.' From these definitions then we must conclude that mediumistic skills cannot be successfully tested in any scientific laboratory, nor measured and monitored with any scientific apparatus. Parapsychologists should be exploring why the mind of a medium is different from the mind of the person with no psychic skills, as opposed to monitoring the phenomena produced by such a mind. I think it should also be understood that psychic abilities are not consistent and do not always work. Whilst training does improve psychic skills, making them much more efficient, results are solely dependent upon the moods and hormonal system of the practitioner. Placing the psychic in the stressful environment of the laboratory makes his or her skills less effective. Furthermore, whilst some psychics may produce positive results under scientific scrutiny, mediumistic results are not so easy to produce.

When is a Medium *not* a Medium?
Knowing which medium to consult when you have lost someone close to you is extremely difficult, particularly when you don't really know exactly what a medium is. Apart from recommendation, all that you can do is randomly select a name from the 'Clairvoyant' column in the local newspaper and hope for the best. Even though I have worked as a professional medium for over 26 years, I have to say that not all mediums are genuine, and even those who are may not be able to give you what you are looking for. Recommendation is not always enough, because what medium is suitable for one person may not necessarily be suitable for another. When you have lost someone close to you the last person to consult is a tarot reader. Visiting a medium who is not genuine, or even a genuine medium who is not quite right for you, can do more harm than good and can sometimes prolong the misery and

pain of bereavement. All mediums have a responsibility to their clients and should always be honest when they have not received anything from the Spirit World. However, the question frequently arises: 'When is a medium not a medium?' to which I always simply reply - 'When he or she is not genuine.' The problem is that a high percentage of mediums who are not genuine are still able to provide what seems like reasonable evidence of survival. And so, the question must arise, if they are not genuine how do they do it?

Although I would be the first to admit when a demonstration of mediumship has not worked, sceptics often criticize me even when the show has been successful, so I can't win either way. It has been suggested that mediums demonstrating in theatres have access to credit card bookings where they make a note of the names and even the addresses of those who have bought tickets. Theatre staff would not allow that to happen, and I'm quite certain that if a medium even suggested such a thing, the show would be called off. Theatres have a legal obligation to their audiences and would not have anything whatsoever to do with any mediumistic trickery. However, there is always the possibility of theatre mediums arranging to have 'plants' in the audience to help guarantee the success of the show. I personally have no knowledge of mediums doing this, but I am quite certain that it does happen. However, I must say that the mediums with whom I have worked over the years have been sincere and genuine.

As I have already said, there are no legal requirements to prevent a person setting up in business as a clairvoyant, nor does any particular Spiritualist body have the monopoly upon mediums. Although mediums can train to certificate standards with the S.N.U, the Spiritualist National Union, and also The Greater World, Christian Spiritualist Association. Until the laws regarding mediums change, no qualifications are legally required to work as a medium or clairvoyant, and this is the problem.

People who Consult Mediums

In my experience as a professional medium I have found there are several kinds of people who consult mediums. (a) The person who has lost someone close. (b) The person who has a general interest in the subject. (c) The person seeking general guidance and therefore misunderstands a medium's true nature. (d) The person who makes a habit of visiting as many mediums as possible. (e) The person who just feels unhealthily drawn towards mediums and psychics, with no particular problem or need.

The latter is perhaps the most dangerous and really the one who should be dissuaded from seeking consultations. Mediums also occasionally encounter the 'Prove it to me' person, who is always willing to waste his money on a consultation, with the sole intention of giving the medium a hard time and proving to all his friends that it's all a load of rubbish. I say 'he' as it's nearly always men who have this attitude. Women appear far more receptive to mediums, whilst the majority of men tend to view them with disdain and cynicism.

It is most definitely true that some people do tend to blow the reading they have had with a particular psychic out of all proportion. In some incidents, the recipient only hears what he or she wants to hear. This may either be positive or negative, and can make the medium seem either absolutely marvellous, or diabolically awful. The majority of working mediums I know mostly get their clientele by recommendation. This means that those who consult them have a fairly good idea of what they can expect. However, I am always reminded of the age old adage, 'Familiarity breeds contempt!' This is certainly the case where mediums and their regular clients are concerned. In fact, I have witnessed this first hand. One business lady had consulted me on a regular basis for over five years, and a lot of people came to me as a result of her recommendation. It got that way that she would not make an important decision without consulting me. In fact, she consulted me for many different things, from business decisions to personal, relationship problems. At one point she was coming to see me every month, and I knew that our friendship would be seriously jeopardized if I said anything to her. Things came to a head when she phoned me to make an appointment, not so long after she had been to see me.

'It's a little too soon,' I stuttered nervously, not wanting to offend her. 'You should really leave it for a while. After all, you only came to see me last week.'

'It won't take long,' she said anxiously. 'I have an important decision to make.'

'Maybe I can help you over the phone,' I stuttered clumsily. 'Save you coming all that way to see me?'

The woman became more and more insistent and I could tell by the tone and urgency of her voice that she was not going to be put off. Against my better judgement, I gave her an appointment that afternoon. When she came into my office I just wanted to get on with the consultation. She, however, wanted to tell me what her problem was and why exactly she wanted to see me. When I told her I didn't want to know, and that I thought it best to see what came out in the reading, she became quite angry. The truth was she wanted me to tell her what she wanted to hear. The problem was to do with her business, and she had already decided what she was going to do long before she walked into my office. When she didn't hear what she wanted to hear she stormed from my office, cursing me as she went. Not only did I not see the woman again, but she made quite certain that her friends stopped consulting me. This is not an isolated incident and I know similar things happen to other mediums. Visiting mediums and clairvoyants on a regular basis can also have its problems for the client as well. There is always the danger that the clairvoyant has remembered everything that has been said in previous consultations, and although the client may have little or no recollection of what has been previously said, most clairvoyants have extremely sharp memories and more than likely will remember. This is not to say that they would dishonestly use information they already have. This is very often done unconsciously, and it is only a minority who would dishonestly pass it back to their client. Nevertheless, it does happen, and those who frequently consult a particular clairvoyant should be warned of what exactly can happen.

Do Psychic Consultations Fulfil a Need?
Even as a professional medium I do have to say that there are occasions when a consultation can do more harm than good, particularly when the client is still grieving for someone who has passed away. Emotions are involved here and the client is very vulnerable. I always feel a need to tread carefully and analyse the information I am receiving before passing it on. A grieving person rarely listens intently and, as a result, he or she will only hear what they want to hear. They only want to know if the person they have lost is alright. The information a medium passes on to the grieving client has to be given gently and with compassion. It has to be specific and must encourage a positive response in the client. So many mediums, particularly the untrained mediums, can be quite clumsy in the way they conduct their consultations. I must say though that even I have been guilty of that, and so great care must always be taken to be gentle and compassionate. A medium must also be mindful that it is just as important for the client to be a good recipient as it is for the medium to be professional and a good medium. Not everyone who consults mediums is a nice, meaningful person. In fact, some clients can be rude and most unpleasant, and as far as they are concerned they are paying you for a service, so they are not obliged to be polite and civil. Generally, though, the majority of those who consult me are quite courteous. I am quite sure that in the majority of cases, private consultations do fulfil a need and can be extremely beneficial. However, there are occasions when a reading with a clairvoyant or medium can be quite emotionally damaging. I am always reminded of one particular case. Nigel Freeberg was a 19-year-old music student with an incredible future ahead of him. Everyone who knew him agreed that he was an extremely talented classical pianist, and someone who had an exceptional aptitude for music. Nigel came from a devoutly Jewish family. Both his parents were doctors and his father was in private practice. Unfortunately, though, Nigel had suffered with depression since he was 12 years-old, and although his condition had been

stabilized by medication, he was still prone to mood swings, which his psychiatrist had put down to the fact that he was sensitive and highly creative. The diagnosis was 'depression with no known cause'. The prognosis for Nigel's psychological condition was uncertain; although his parents were assured that he would most probably grow out of it.

Although Nigel was quite religious, and attended the synagogue with his father every week, he began showing an interest in Spiritualism. Without his parents' knowledge he secretly attended the local Spiritualist Church with a friend every Tuesday evening. As a result of the 'messages' he had received from various mediums, Nigel began seeking ways of developing his own psychic abilities. He was a medium, he had been told, and he was being guided by a North American Indian. He joined a 'development circle' in the Spiritualist Church, in the hope of cultivating his sensitivity and strengthening his relationship with his Spirit Guide. Within a very short space of time his whole personality changed; he became irrational and extremely hyperactive, and would go for walks in the early hours of the morning simply to 'unwind'. Although his parents were extremely loving, they appeared to be oblivious to his behaviour and simply left him to his own devices. Unfortunately, though, Nigel decided to get a Ouija Board, and began using it in his room every night. Whatever happened in his room on Friday 13th May, caused Nigel to take his pet dog Marly for a walk to the local park, somewhere around 9.30pm. The last person to see him alive was Fran Dolan, a neighbour and family friend. Nigel was discovered face down in the park lake early the following morning. Marly, his dog, was found waiting patiently on the grassy bank. Although the coroner had said that Nigel's mind had been disturbed at the time he committed suicide, in his summing up his final conclusion was that Spiritualism had obviously influenced his clouded judgment and ultimately encouraged him to do what he did. This is so often the case. In fact, I always discourage anyone with psychological or emotional problems from getting involved in the process of psychic development or anything to do with the paranormal. Alan Kardec, Spiritist and writer of many early books on the supernatural, such as *The Medium's Book*, and *The Spirit's Book,* often suggested that development of psychic abilities could possibly cause insanity. I have always believed that this is true when a person is psychologically unbalanced. When insanity is there potentially, the cultivation of the psychic faculties can encourage a full breakdown. Should that happen to a person who is involved with Spiritualism, then that religion is brought into disrepute. Although Spiritualism is recognized by Parliament as a religion, it is still not fully accepted and has always been perceived as one of those 'odd' religions with a cultist following.

The Truth about Mediums?

Although I have been a professional medium for over twenty five years I fully understand why psychics and mediums receive so much criticism from sceptics etc. Regardless of what mediums and psychics say about their abilities, these sorts of skills do not stand up to scientific or psychological scrutiny. In fact, mediums who willingly offer themselves for examination in a controlled scientific environment, I do feel really leave themselves wide open to ridicule. Nor can I see the point of offering one's services to help the police locate a missing person, or even to apprehend the perpetrator of a crime, when the methods employed are so 'hit and miss' and very rarely produce positive results. Why would a medium offer his or her services in this way, other than for the publicity they hope it will bring? The way in which mediums are today portrayed is the primary reason why I have become even more sceptical and extremely critical of the whole mediumistic arena, and I think that today the majority of mediums hang themselves out to dry so that the proverbial wolves can devour them. Long before I decided to professionally use my psychic skills, I made a point of visiting as many mediums and psychics as possible, and did in actual fact see well in the region of four thousand all over the UK. I must say that the mediums who impressed me the most in those early years failed to do so once I had begun working as a medium myself. Arrogance and vanity wrongly led me to believe that this was simply because my mediumship was far superior to theirs. However, in reality it was simply a case that I had learnt all of the tricks of the trade, so to speak, and therefore knew exactly how they were working and using their abilities. Before beginning this project with Ciarán I had already decided that in order for it to be worthwhile and interesting to the general public, I had to be perfectly truthful about my skills and the skills of my peers. Whilst I believe that I am a very genuine and honest medium, I also know that mediumistic skills are extremely unreliable, even with the best intentions. Therefore, it would be quite unfair to make a judgement about a medium after one demonstration. Even so, I can honestly say that although I do have the greatest of respect for some close mediumistic friends, I have not been impressed by the abilities of any mediums I have seen working today. I recently went to see one particular medium working in a local Wirral hall. The advert he placed in the local paper read something like this: *'One of the UK's most evidential mediums. First and second names and addresses given.'* What on earth is that all about? The medium in question used to attend my annual seminars in Liverpool, and as far as I was aware, he was not an aspiring medium and did not have any interest in becoming a medium. His job was in advertising and marketing, and he even left a comment in the seminar's visiting book: *'More marketing needed.'* As far as I now know he is making a comfortable living appearing in halls etc all over the North West. Other mediums advertise themselves in this way: *'The accuracy of his messages will astound you! One of the UK's most evidential mediums.'* The popular television programme *Most Haunted* used to invite veritably unknown mediums to guest on the programme, who would sometimes attempt to mimic the insane antics of the programme's resident medium, front man, Derek Acorah. However, the majority of the mediums appearing would always seize the opportunity to use their appearance on the programme in their promotional blurb. For example: *'As seen on Most Haunted…'* Even though they had made only one or two appearances on the programme. Pioneering Spiritualist and journalist, Hannon Swaffer, once said: "No publicity is bad," a statement with which I had always disagreed until it was proved very wrong by a particular celebrity medium. I have to reluctantly say that there are those celebrity mediums who have gone from strength to strength, in spite of the adverse publicity they received in some national newspapers and elsewhere. All that this proves to me is that the television channels, or production companies, that employ such mediums are not really interested in whether or not they are a genuine medium. As long as the viewing figures are consistently maintained, nothing else matters. The problem is one of definition. The media - television in particular - do not have any understanding of mediumship and what it is really about. It is true that in order for it to be good viewing, the paranormal has to be entertaining. However, the problem I have with the way it is presented on the numerous television programmes is the sensationalism. This give a completely wrong idea to the viewing public who expect all mediums to be like the ones they see on television.

Today, primarily because of the way mediums and psychics are presented on television and radio, the general public does not fully understand what a medium actually is. As I have said elsewhere, a medium's job is to prove the continuity of the soul beyond death. No medium - no matter who they are - possesses the power to 'call' anyone back. By its very nature, mediumship does not always work. I find it an extremely unreliable process, and one which is completely out of the medium's control. When a medium is consulted by someone who has been recently bereaved, it really should be made clear from the very beginning of the consultation that the so-called dead person may simply not be there to communicate with the medium. Or, as sometimes is the case, the dead person may not want to communicate. This may come as a surprise to many people, but not all disembodied spirits want to communicate with those still living in the corporeal world, particularly if they do not have too many happy memories of his or her life. Also, the process of communication is sometimes alien to some individuals once they have passed over; and even with their best intentions, passing on information to a mediumistically inclined individual becomes daunting and an extremely complicated process. In such cases a third party may be required, and so a discarnate intermediary is frequently called upon. So-called Spirit Guides do make sense, even though the archetypal 'Red Indian' Spirit Guide is often looked at with some disdain and ridiculed by those not privy to Spiritualist beliefs.

Mediums in the Security of the Spiritualist Church

With the exception of a few, the majority of mediums have done their training in the Spiritualist church circuit. Although demonstrating mediumistic skills in a Spiritualist church can sometimes be quite daunting, it's still a lot easier than demonstrating in a theatre or any other venue outside the safety of Spiritualism. Many times I have attended Spiritualist meetings and watched with amazement as the demonstrating medium has delivered messages to a congregation consisting of people he or she has personally known. In fact, on one occasion the medium referred to the recipient of her message by name, and then proceeded to deliver information that they had previously been talking about before the meeting. It went something like this: 'Can I talk to you, Margaret? I've got Tommy here. He's saying you should spend the money on yourself and buy that coat you like.' Anyone attending for the first time would be quite impressed. However, little would they know that the medium knew practically everyone in the congregation. Mediums who travel the length and breadth of the UK to serve Spiritualist churches do very often get to know the regulars of the churches by name. I'm not suggesting that all mediums working on the spiritualist Church circuit would work in this way, but what I am saying is many Spiritualist mediums do exploit their personal knowledge of church members in this way. Later on I'd like to ask Ciarán a question related to this and his experience witnessing Gordon Smith demonstrate in a Spiritualist Church.

Over twenty years ago now I received a phone call from a friend who needed to see me as a matter of great urgency. In fact, even though it was around ten pm, it sounded so important I agreed for him to call my home. When he arrived he was accompanied by a lady who eventually became a working medium at Stansted Hall, the Spiritualist

National Union College of Studies. The matter they so urgently wanted to discuss with me was in fact to tell me "We do not think you should be working as a medium, but as a teacher." This, they assured me, had come directly from the Spirit World. The lady in question eventually ran a hotel in North Wales, devoted primarily to seminars and workshops for anyone seeking to develop their own mediumistic skills. She occasionally worked for me at Woolton Hall in the suburb of Liverpool. On one particular occasion I received two complaints that she had been seen hanging round the women's toilets, and that she had been listening to a conversation between two friends, the personal contents of which she used when giving a message to one of them. They were quite disgusted, and to safeguard my own reputation, I never used the alleged medium again. Nonetheless, she is still working as a medium within the confines of the Spiritualist movement, and still travels all over the world.

A few months before the late and great Doris Stokes passed away, her manager, Laurie O'Leary invited me to compare one of her shows at the Crucible Theatre in Sheffield. I spent the day with Doris in her hotel suite, whilst her manager gave me my instructions for the evening. As was always the case with Doris Stokes, the theatre had sold out a few days before, and there was an estimated audience of somewhere in the region of 2000 people expected. After Laurie had finished explaining the running order of the show to me, he turned his attention to Doris. I was somewhat shocked when he mentioned some of the names of people who would be in the audience, and even reminded her of the deceased people they would be expecting to hear from. "Oh, I remember him," said Doris. "Paul Strachen is the young man who wears his grandmother's locket that has some of his own baby hair in?"

"That's right!" smiled Laurie. "If you get stuck just call on him." He then went on to remind her of a woman whose brother had been shot, and although the coroner had given an open verdict, the whole family believed that he had been murdered by his partner. "So, if you have any difficulties whatsoever," he went assured her, "these people will help you out, ok, Doll?"

I thought I was hearing things, and couldn't believe that Doris Stokes would resort to such things to make her show work. I was even more shocked when, during the evening's demonstration I heard Doris call out, "Paul Strachen! Is there someone called Paul Strachen in the audience?" And a young man put his hand up and waited patiently for Doris to pass on a message to him from his dead grandmother. I heard Doris repeat everything I had heard Laurie O'Leary say to her in the hotel room during the day. And so the evening went on. I'm not saying that nothing was genuine about her demonstration that night. On the contrary, there were other very evidential messages. But I did later wonder. I was once told that when a medium reaches a certain high standard of popularity and fame, that has to be maintained no matter what. As I have previously said, mediumship is extremely unreliable and most certainly does not always work. Faced with a theatre full of eager faces that have paid to see a demonstration of mediumship, what does one do when there is nothing happening? I once stood before a capacity theatre in Southport when such a thing happened to me. Although I struggled through the show, I vowed that I would not allow it to happen again. This was the reason I developed Psychic Handwriting Analysis, a psychic method of divination from which I could glean information about the writer's past, present and future. Although it was just a crutch to help me when a mediumistic demonstration was not going according to plan, audiences seemed to thoroughly enjoy it.

Mediums Galore!
When I was a small boy my mother used to take me to a wool shop on the High Street that was run by two elderly sisters. Upon entering the shop my mother would say to the lady behind the counter 'I've come for the meeting,' and she would then be shown into a back room where a Spiritualist service would be held. In those days Spiritualism was in fact one of those 'odd' religions that was spoken of in hushed tones. Because Spiritualism, as a religion was in its embryonic stages, it

was quite furtive and nearly always viewed with some caution, and often referred to as the 'spooks'. Although today it is much more widely accepted as a religion, it is still not really regarded as being equal with the other main religions of the world, and still receives a great deal of criticism from the general public. Spiritualism is a religion according to an act of Parliament in the early 1950s. In fact, Cosmo Lang, Archbishop of the Church of England in 1936, received so many letters of complaints about Spiritualism and its unusual claims, that he appointed a committee of ten signatories to investigate it. The committee was made up of people from all walks of life, who in fact investigated Spiritualism and what went on within the confines of the Spiritualist Church. The report was in fact secreted away for ten years, its findings not being made public. Eventually though the *Psychic News*, the leading journal of Spiritualism, eventually got hold of the report and published it. It was called 'The Majority Report', and stated very clearly that, if we were to disregard the phenomena of Spiritualism, Clairvoyance, Mediumship and healing, then we have to disregard the phenomena of the New Testament, which was exactly the same. Whether it was as a direct result of the Majority Report or not, in 1952 Spiritualism was made a recognized religion by an act of parliament. This actually meant that Spiritualist meetings no longer had to be conducted in the shadows and those who had an interest in Spiritualism no longer had to hide the fact that they did. The pioneers of Spiritualism had succeeded, the door of the Spiritualist Church was now wide open, and everyone invited. However, today this is all 'old hat', so to speak, and there are Spiritualist churches everywhere. Although this is the case, the primary attraction of Spiritualism is in fact the demonstration of mediumship. If we were to remove such phenomena from the Spiritualist Service then I am quite confident that the churches would be quite empty. The general public are only interested in the phenomena, and very often greatly misunderstand what the role of a medium actually is. Because of the lack of education about the aims of Spiritualism and its mediumistic ambassadors, people very often wrongly think that, as well as receiving information from the so-called dead, mediums also foretell the future. This is a very wrong assumption. A medium is a person who endeavours, or should endeavour, to prove the continuity of the soul beyond death, no more and no less. Predicting the future events of someone's life should be left to the skills of a fortune teller or Tarot card reader. Today there are more mediums than there are people interested in spiritualism. There are mediums galore, not only in the many Spiritualist Churches all over the world, but also demonstrating their abilities in theatres, hotel function rooms, on radio and on television. Mediums that have never been heard of before are suddenly appearing. The whole mediumistic profession has gone quite crazy, and it is now impossible for anyone to know which medium is good or which one is even genuine; it's all trial and error, often at great expense.

Is it Healthy to Visit Mediums Regularly?

Although I have mentioned this a little earlier in the book, I think because of the serious nature of the whole subject, the point is worthy of another mention. I have said before that some people live their lives by what mediums tell them. Frequently those who have had a private consultation with me will ask, 'When do you think it is ok for me to come again?' This is a question that really doesn't require an answer. The truth is, if any medium has done his or her job well, and the reading has been quite evidential, then a further consultation should not be necessary. Consulting a clairvoyant for futuristic guidance is a little different. However, even then I do think it's unwise to consult psychics and clairvoyants too frequently. Some people are extremely emotionally vulnerable and can be psychologically damaged if the person he or she is consulting is inexperienced. The majority of mediums I know do have professional morals and a code of ethics to which they work. However, there is a minority of unscrupulous so-called 'psychics', whose sole intention it is to make money and, with very little care of how this is achieved. In saying this, I do have a fairly regular and very loyal clientele, some of whom visit me at least once a year, often just for some spiritual guidance. I do work both as a medium and as a psychic. At the risk of repeating myself, mediumistic skills are unreliable and therefore do not always work. Sometimes I look upon my psychic skills as a sort of lever or even a platform that I am able to use to support my mediumistic abilities.

Chapter 8
Question Time - Part 2
The Parapsychologist questions the Clairvoyant - Ciarán asks Billy

Interesting that you mention 'Corner of the Eye Syndrome'. You relate it to 'psychic apparitions' yet the same phenomena are used by psychologists specializing in visual perception to give a normal explanation for witnesses of ghosts. Do you think we're just interpreting the same thing differently? Is there common ground with these particular phenomena?

Billy answers: Although I know there are medical reasons why we experience the 'Corner of the Eye Syndrome', with these the light forms and images perceived, are mostly quite nebulous shapes without definition. (Sense?) When the visual response mechanism produces genuine Spirit 'side images', they are extremely clear and have a significant effect upon the image-making faculty of the brain. When the images experienced with the so-called Corner of the Eye Syndrome, are genuine spirit forms they do not persist for any great length of time, but are very often quite fleeting. When anything else is the cause this is absolutely not the case, and the images remain there until the 'seer' looks directly at them. On the occasions I have experienced these sorts of phenomena, the 'side images' disappear to leave a clearly defined impression in my brain. These are usually extremely quite animated with vivid shapes and defined features. So I do not believe we are interpreting the same phenomenon differently. I am quite sure that we are talking about two completely different phenomena, even though the two are produced by the same visual response mechanism.

Why are some of these names that you gave earlier, 'incredible psychic artists'? Was it more than the art being incredible? Do you have testimonials of accurate drawings that could not have been obtained via one of the normal five senses?

Billy answers: I always work on the premise that 'seeing is believing'. I have had personal proof from Ivor James in the form of a drawing of my father (whom Ivor did not know) who died in 1970. Ivor gave me personal information about my father that left both my mother and myself astounded. I have also witnessed Coral Polge sketching my friend's mother who had recently passed on. The information she gave, combined with a life-like sketch, totally convinced me that she had received all that she gave from a discarnate source. Let's not forget that mediumistic messages are quite personal to those to whom they are given, and quite meaningless to everyone else. A medium is only as good as the responses they receive.

Your concept of the Spirit World is fascinating but it is what we call in science - an unfalsifiable hypothesis. This means that there is no way I can prove you wrong, or right, until I die. I just have to take your word for it. So why should I believe in your concept of the Spirit World, and not others?

Billy answers: It is an axiom of physics that no two bodies of matter can occupy the same space without in any way interfering with each other. But millions upon millions of vibrations can exist in the same space, at the same time, without affecting each other in any way whatsoever. This is a scientific fact and also a metaphysical concept. We most certainly live in a multidimensional world in which there are worlds within worlds, each rising in a gradually ascending vibratory scale, from those which touch and blend with the highest physical planes, to those which gradually merge with the lowest spiritual planes. The Spirit world is not a place; it is a condition or state of being. Remember, "In my Father's House are many mansions." What He was speaking about were states of vibrations.

Do you recommend everyone does some form of meditation?
Billy answers: Yes, I do. Meditation is an extremely efficient way of promoting serenity and calmness and making the mind more focused. Certain kinds of meditation encourage equilibrium of body, mind and spirit. Mediums should be encouraged to meditate on a daily basis. I learned to meditate in the sixties, and cultivated my own technique of Yantric and pranayamic meditation. These methods helped me in my own life.

We did some interesting tests together in the lab. The results of the geo-graphic profiling study (a medium, a profiler and a student) showed that the geographic profiler did best and then on 2 out of 7 of the cases you beat the student. Again, following on from a previous question in the first dialogue, why is your ability not consistent?
Billy answers: It is a case of 'horses for courses' to use a cliché. What the majority of psychics fail to understand is that he or she has to have an aptitude for a particular area. Just because a psychic regards himself as being very accurate does not mean that he or she has the ability to find missing persons. In my case I would prefer to actually be 'on scene'. This is where my skills would be most efficient. Although I can do psychometry I really don't have the aptitude for it. In other words, the process is 'hit and miss' for me. My psychic skills are inconsistent because my heart has to be in it. Mediumistic skills are not reliable, simply because no medium can guarantee communication. In other words, mediums cannot call anyone back. The whole mediumistic process is purely experimental - it doesn't always work!

Do you think it's perhaps dangerous for psychics/mediums to get involved in criminal investigations?
Billy answers: I don't think it's dangerous for psychics and mediums to be involved in criminal investigations, but in the majority of cases it can be misleading and often gives the whole profession a bad name.

Do you find it difficult to separate your emotions from your work? Is it tiring?

Billy answers: My work is extremely tiring, and often depressing. I frequently find it difficult to separate myself emotionally from what I am doing. I think all mediums are the same. If they say otherwise they're telling lies. As I get older I find my work increasingly more difficult and much more draining. It makes me irritable and very depressed. It makes me look closer at my own mortality.

Reading through everything you've written about so far, I really want to know how you feel about the crystal ball, Ouija etc. Is there any need for the use of 'gimmicks'?

Billy answers: I have always advocated the use of scrying techniques and divinatory tools such as the crystal speculum. I have used the crystal ball since I was very young. I use it as a tool with which to focus the attention. The crystal speculum, black mirror, burning candle are all excellent tools with which to cultivate the faculties. I am totally opposed to the Ouija board. This encourages instability and often attracts the vagabond element from the lower astral. Look what's happened to Degsy!

The Clairvoyant questions The Parapsychologist - Billy asks Ciarán

I would like to know exactly how you feel about the way in which mediums are portrayed on television, and do you see yourself as prostituting your own profession as a psychologist by taking part in the histrionics and theatrics exhibited on programmes like Most Haunted?

Ciarán answers: Firstly, regarding the television portrayal of mediums - how mediums are portrayed is to do with motivation, motivation of television production companies and the motivation of the medium involved. An hour's televised clairvoyant demonstration from a spiritualist church would not necessarily be the most exciting programme. Viewers would witness 'hits' and 'misses' and messages that, although significant for the intended recipients, would seem mundane to a TV audience. The way mediums are portrayed on television, in my opinion, is partly down to sensationalism and editing and perhaps, to some extent, in response to ratings. The rest of it, in my opinion, is down to how the medium works and how comfortable they are in becoming more dramatic for the cameras if it is required. Some mediums deliver messages in a matter of fact manner, others are vague and ambiguous, others go into trance and yet others change facial expression and their voices when channelling. Your concerns about the portrayal of mediums and how a show like *Most Haunted* may have damaged the reputation, or perception, of mediums is one view. Additionally it may have given rise to every 'Tom, Dick and Mary' who thinks they can use their untapped 'ability' for financial gain or to genuinely help people, or just to know more. Another is that paranormal programmes have brought mediumship to the forefront again, have made it acceptable and popular. Despite clients turning up at your door expecting you to do a 'Derek', have you ever been as busy or had so many people show an interest? We haven't seen an interest in mediumship like this since the late 1800s, early 1900s. For some that's a bad thing, for others not.

Secondly, regarding my involvement on programmes like *Most Haunted*. No I don't think I'm prostituting my profession. Remember that I do wear many hats. My academic research speaks for itself - conference presentations, articles in peer-reviewed journals, lectures etc. I was originally brought onto the show to give the sceptical voice, to offer alternative explanations for any alleged phenomena. Sceptics on paranormal shows frequently suffer from the usual treatment, which is they are wheeled on at the end wearing a shirt and tie, looking all academic, to quash any paranormal thoughts. They are frequently portrayed as the spoilsport and fit into a segment in the programme where viewers leave the comfort of their sofas and head into the kitchen to put the kettle on. The sort of comments I've heard in the past are "He's never got anything new to say," "He's always down on the paranormal," "Doesn't matter what he says, I still believe," etc. Joining the *Most Haunted* team gave me the opportunity to change that perception a bit. Viewers hear the sceptical side whilst immersed in the excitement of being in a haunted house. Also, I find that some of the sceptical explanations are getting through to the masses (e.g. orbs are not paranormal, EMF meters are not ghost detectors, there's always an alternative explanation). In terms of your use of the words 'histrionics' and 'theatrics' to describe the show, there certainly is that element but remember that what you are ultimately seeing is an hour's edited footage taken from over a 100 hours of raw footage. The investigative method used is only one approach; if I were running the show, yes, it might be different, but let me ask you this. Is an hour of watching two people sitting in a darkened room entertaining? Is 30 minutes of a camera locked off on a trigger object stimulating television?

Gordon Smith, hailed as the UK's most accurate medium, worked for a short while on Most Haunted. Although you seemed to respect Gordon's mediumship, you were really only impressed by the content of his messages when you saw him work in a Spiritualist Church in London. You used the word 'impressive'. I would like to ask you why you think this was? You did say to me

at the time that you thought he was more comfortable in that environment. I'm not making any suggestions, but I would like to point out that Gordon Smith is a regular visitor to that church.

Ciarán answers: My respect for Gordon's mediumship came out of the work that he conducted with Archie Roy and Tricia Robertson. Their extensive attempts to test mediumship lasted several years and employed many controls in an attempt to ensure there was no natural explanation for accurate messages should they come through. It's true everything I said about Gordon. I did get the impression that he was more comfortable demonstrating in the church rather than on television. I did also use the word 'impressive' in regards to his demonstration. This was because his style was very different to other mediums I had seen in Spiritualist Churches. There was nothing vague and ambiguous about the messages and they were short, to the point and immediately directed to particular members of the congregation. Your observation about him being a regular *is* a suggestion at a valid alternative explanation. Again, as I've said before, assessing whether you're actually witnessing paranormal communication has to be a personal decision and for me, unless we can be certain there is no other explanation for what is going on, I remain sceptical.

I have heard you frequently say that you have never seen any evidence of mediumistic ability in any medium, but in all your years as a parapsychologist have you ever seen any evidence of metaphysical skills in anyone?

Ciarán answers: I find the use of the word 'metaphysics' nowadays to mean pretty much anything beyond the physical world. It is a philosophical term that has been abducted by the New Age movement and, as such, I think it has lost its original meaning. Originally it was a philosophy concerned with principles of reality beyond science, the idea of necessity, determinism and free will (essentially a philosophy explaining the nature of being and the world). There are true metaphysicists out there, yes. Philosophers who study ontology or theology are essentially metaphysicists. But in terms of your question I think you're referring to any skills 'beyond the physical world'. The answer, no. Let me rephrase that, I have met a few people who have claimed to have metaphysical skills (gurus, healers, shamans), but they've either performed badly under test conditions or have provided evidence of their skill in the real world where I remain sceptical. Fascinated, but sceptical.

Do you really think that the veteran mediums of Spiritualism were any different to the mediums of the Spiritualism today? Has anything really changed about mediums other than the fact that today they can demonstrate their skills in theatres and hotel function rooms?

Ciarán answers: The big change for me has been the reduction in physical mediumship. The veteran mediums of Spiritualism managed to produce physical evidence of Spirit (e.g. rapping, apports, ectoplasm, spirit manifestation, levitation etc) on a regular basis. That doesn't happen now with the same frequency as back then. I think there's good alternative explanations for why that is and it's to do with the advent of night vision cameras, the development of magic and fakery knowledge and the fact that so many mediums were being caught faking physical phenomena. There are still, to this day, however, the very rare cases that confound critics (e.g. D. D. Home, 1833-1886). In recent years the only reported physical phenomena of note has been the Scole Group, and I encourage interested readers to consult a copy of the Scole Report (from the SPR) and draw their own conclusions. In terms of mental mediumship, I don't think much has changed, just the venue. Whereas before Spiritualist mediums would relay messages in public and private séances in a parlour or front room (sometimes theatres) or demonstrate in early Spiritualist Churches, now Spiritualist mediums can be found running workshops in specialized colleges, filling theatres, authoring blogs on the web, writing columns in magazines or newspapers, appearing on television and demonstrating in the 400+ Spiritualist Churches in the UK (and more elsewhere in the world). The messages, however, are still the same and are delivered in the same way.

As an aside, I do make the distinction between Spiritualist mediums and mediums and I stand by my answer as you do find Spiritualist mediums in every 'medium', for want of a better word.

What would convince you of mediumship ability? What would convince you of something paranormal?

Ciarán answers: That is a tough one. Two questions though. The first is logically impossible. Even if a medium provided information to me, or someone else, under controlled conditions, about a departed relative or friend, that I knew nothing about, it still wouldn't be proof. The information would either remain unknown, therefore leaving the door of doubt open, or would be verified somewhere down the line. If it is verified then someone has knowledge of it and so there's always the alternative explanation that it is another form of paranormal communication, not mediumship. Additionally the information would have to be so specific to exclude the possibility of a high probability statement and of me reading into what was given. Alternatively, even if a medium apported, in front of me, a personal object linked to a departed relative, the circumstances would have to be so well controlled that I don't think any medium would agree to them.

What would convince me of something paranormal? I used to say that if an apparition appeared in front of me I would be convinced*. Now being aware of issues associated with visual hallucinations etc, I would have to have the event verified by a second independent witness and filmed using two different cameras.

Aside from any personal experience I may have there are mountains of eyewitness accounts from eminent scientists and members of the public in the early Proceedings of the Society for Psychical Research. Accounts of haunting experiences, séance room phenomena, mediumistic messages and telepathy etc. Also there are programmes of research into various aspects of parapsychological phenomena (e.g. micro PK, telepathy in a Ganzfeld environment etc). This wealth of information would make anybody wonder and question whether sceptics have really put forward convincing arguments, and proof of natural explanations, for different alleged phenomena. What do you think?

* Thanks to Steve Parsons of Para.Science for pointing out the weakness in my original statement.

Chapter 9
Divination methods - Scrying, Ouija Board, Astrology

The Parapsychologist - Ciarán O'Keeffe
Introduction to Divination
Divination is commonly defined as the art or practice of seeking information about future events or discovering hidden knowledge (i.e. what is unknown) usually by interpreting signs. It is derived from the Greek word μαντεια, which itself comes from the word μαντις meaning 'seer'. The Catholic Encyclopaedia explains that seeking knowledge about these two things requires a special power. If you think about, there is some logic in this as gaining knowledge about the future through normal means is inadequate and so, according to the Encyclopaedia, power given by either gods or evil spirits is required. The same argument is used for the discovery of 'hidden' or 'unknown' knowledge though the exact nature of this type of knowledge is unclear. Is it names, dates and personal facts hidden in the recesses of a client's mind? Is it information about a family member previously unknown to the seer or client? Is it some ancient secret Knowledge that has been buried over the centuries by ignorant faiths and scientists? (Don't get me started on The Secret!) The implication is that it could be any of these things. Once you start to examine the different divination methods you realize that perhaps the sort of knowledge you're after depends on what method you use and there are lots of methods.

Cicero, the Roman philosopher (and statesman, lawyer, prose stylist, political theorist, and public speaker!), categorized divining methods into two types - natural and artificial. Natural divining is largely untaught and unskilled and includes methods like dreams and oracles. In this context the diviner is merely passive and the prediction or knowledge simply occurs requiring no interpretation. Artificial divining, on the other hand, is sometimes taught but certainly requires some observation and interpretation skill. It is comprised of fortune telling from signs found in nature or manmade. Here the diviner is an active subject and the divination comes apparently from their own skill and observation. To make this clearer and to classify some methods of divination that you've heard of, I've further subdivided them into three types (or 'classes' as they are referred to in the Encyclopedia of Occultism and Parapsychology). The first one is the same as Cicero's 'natural' divination whereas the other two are 'artificial' in terms of requiring skill in interpreting:

* **First class** *(Express or Explicit invocation)*: necromancy (using spirits of the dead); oneiromancy (divination by dreams); Pythonism (or receiving divinatory messages from the possessed); hydromancy (signs in water) or scrying; aeromancy (signs in air); crystal gazing; radiesthesia (use of a pendulum); automatic writing; Ouija, etc.

* **Second class** *(Tacit or Implicit invocation - natural signs)*: a good example of this is genethliacal astrology; or palmistry (otherwise known as chiromancy); augury (the flight of birds); or chance meeting with ominous animals, etc.

* **Third class** *(Tacit invocation - manmade signs)*: includes geomancy from points or lines on paper or pebbles thrown at random (e.g. runes); throwing dice; the use of cards (e.g. Tarot or other forms of cartomancy); opening a book at random (or bibliomancy which is more generally the use of books in divination), etc.

There are numerous others not listed above, some you've heard of (e.g. I Ching which is considered a form of bibliomancy) and others you've probably not (e.g. extispicy - looking for signs in the entrails of animals as opposed to haruspicy, which is specifically concerned with the entrails of animals who have been sacrificed!). Bibliomancy is an ancient form of divination that seems to have existed since books were first published. 'Sortes Virgilianae', for example, is fortune telling using Virgil's *Aeneid* (written in the 1st century BC) and verses and words from the Bible have often been given prophetic significance.

Divination is practically as old as the human race. It is found in every historical period and culture, (e.g. among the Egyptians, Mayans, Hindus, Romans, and Greeks). Historically, the Burmese would divine by piercing an egg at each end, blowing the contents onto the ground then interpreting outlines of things to be. In Peru, diviners predicted the future by examining the leaves of tobacco, the shapes of maize grains, or even the paths of spiders. The tribes of Northern Asia had their shamans, the Celts their druids, Native American Indians their medicine-men - all were recognized diviners. Even though it has historical weight behind it, however, it doesn't make it any more genuine.

The Clairvoyant - Billy Roberts
Introductory Warning

The use of any methods to heighten the awareness can very often precipitate specific changes in the brain, thus causing the nervous system to be overloaded. Should a person have a history of psychological or emotional disorders, then anything used to cultivate the powers of the mind could be detrimental to the psychological health. For an example, using a Ouija Board may not only encourage the closeness of unsavoury spirits and discarnate vagabonds, but could also interfere with the overall balance of the person's mind. The process of psychic development encourages the cultivation of the senses and heightens the awareness. Should the practitioner not be psychologically and spiritually prepared then nervous overload frequently occurs. As a consequence of not being emotionally grounded, many working mediums have nervous breakdowns. In fact, there is a high percentage of mediums who are quite nervous and either smoke or drink too much. Mediumistic skills operate on an extremely high frequency of nervous energy, and as a consequence of this process mediums often appear quite unhealthy, either physically or emotionally. I am quite sure that many mediums will dismiss this as being ridiculous. However, I must say that I have researched the subject for over 25 years and have found that out of 1000 mediums only 75 proved to be fairly healthy and psychologically well balanced. When I am feeling a little psychologically low, it has a profound effect upon my mediumship. Unless I take a break from using my skills when I am like that, I become extremely depressed and find it very difficult to dispel the dark cloud that follows me around for weeks. I am quite sure that the majority of mediums experience similar mental states and may not even realize what's causing it. Mediums are supposed to be psychologically grounded and most definitely well balanced. I am not sure whether there is such an entity as a well balanced medium, as mediumship, by its very nature, functions within a fairly unbalanced mind.

My approach to psychic development is holistic, and before the part can be looked at the whole must be explored. For the above reasons I do not allow simply anyone to enrol on a course at my centre. Before we consider new applicants a psychological profile is done. The whole person is considered. Should I suspect that he or she is in anyway unbalanced, then I politely discourage them from getting involved, at least for the time being.

The Parapsychologist - Ciarán O'Keeffe
Scrying

Scrying is commonly defined as the occult practice of traditionally using a reflective surface or translucent body to aid psychic abilities. It comes from an old English word, *descry,* meaning 'to make out dimly' or 'to reveal'. My understanding of the process, having experimented with it in numerous haunted locations, is that the reflective surface acts as an attention focus. It removes unwanted thoughts and distractions and allows you to free associate, eventually allowing you evoke any internal images onto the reflective surface. It is, therefore, extremely successful in an environment of calm and low level lighting where the point of focus can be distorted, visually, and therefore actually create pictures in much the same way as looking at an ink blot for a period of time reveals different images.

It's not a new concept. There are references to this form of 'communication' as far back as ancient Egypt (i.e. 3,000 BC) and ancient Greece (around 2,000BC). In fact, there is mention of the scrying method in some of Homer's texts. In one particular scene the main character digs a hole, fills it with lamb's blood and attempts to make contact with a departed spirit in order to seek wisdom about his future. This method is also referred to in Raymond Moody's books on the after-life. He is the author who developed the 'psychomanteum' - a pitch black cabinet where you sit and stare up at a mirror, attempting to contact a departed loved one.

Interestingly, I did actually sit in a psychomanteum at the Rhine Research Center in North Carolina back in 2000. I was there as part of a summer research program on parapsychology, kind of like a 'summer school', where we were given lectures and workshops by some of the most highly respected individuals in the field. A member of staff, who had been trained by the well-known Diane Arcangel, gave us an insight into the psychomanteum, its history, development and use as a bereavement counselling tool. We were encouraged to participate in a session and so I threw myself into the opportunity wholeheartedly. In the lengthy induction phase I discussed the departed relative I hoped to contact, then listened to the instructions and prepared for the session. Once seated in the actual psychomanteum I completely relaxed. Think of it like a blacked out photo booth where you're sitting in a really comfortable chair that's too low to see your reflection. A very low-level external light source ensures that you see a very slight reflection of the psychomanteum wall in the mirror in front of you, but slightly above your eye-line. Your eyes take time to focus and get adjusted to the dark and even when you start to focus on the mirror and its reflection you find your eyes slip in and out of focus. Despite my expectations, I had a momentary flash of a friend who had passed away a few years before. I began to reflect on his life and the time in which I knew him, realizing I had never grieved for him. It was a rewarding experience and in the debrief I was told it was the sort of experience one would expect. I don't think anything paranormal or any sort of divination had occurred, it was a perfect case of priming and the psychology of the process. Despite this, the fact that I was assisted by a trained bereavement counsellor made it a positive and very insightful experience.

Psychological Problems

Whether psychological problems arise out of using such divinatory methods is difficult to ascertain. There is certainly no academic or scientific research to show that there are psychological problems that could arise as a result of this form of communication, or, should I say, aide to communication. The difficultly arises in assessing the truth. A teenager, for example, could easily get into scrying and, without, proper supervision, could go down the route of those vulnerable few who have delved into Ouija. They could become addicted. The problem is that the addiction could be fuelled by apparent success using scrying, yet, the communications may be simple confabulations (i.e. from their mind). In addition, remember my personal experience with the psychomanteum that I discussed earlier. Imagine the same situation happening (using any scrying method) to someone without a counsellor present, or to someone without knowledge of the alternative explanations. What would be the psychological impact of such an experience?

The Clairvoyant - Billy Roberts

Some schools of thought believe that even crystal ball scrying can be dangerous and may attract unwanted discarnate energies. I must admit that I used a crystal speculum for many years, as a means of focusing my attention. This method was favoured by the ancient seers, who would use the crystal sphere to glean all sorts of information, particularly as a means of obtaining knowledge of the future. I used the crystal speculum as a tool with which to focus my mind and to encourage the cultivation of my awareness.

What do you See?
Although I used the crystal speculum primarily as a tool for meditation, I did see quite a lot. The images I saw in the crystal were extremely vivid and clear, and not at all nebulous or vague. It was like watching a scene from a movie,, and although the images made absolutely no sense to me, I would sit for long periods, totally enthralled. However, I must say that the crystal ball merely acted as a focal point or screen for what was processed in my mind.

How does it Work?
The process of scrying actually causes the retina of the eyes to be anaesthetized. In other words, the vision goes out of focus and the eyes begin to tear. At this point the image-making faculty of the brain becomes active, encouraging the subconscious mind to process and release images stored in its own memory chambers.

Does this Exercise cause any Psychological Problems?
Should there be a propensity towards psychological problems, I am quite sure it can do. Although I have always considered myself to be fairly well balanced, psychologically speaking, the whole exercise did cause some problems for me. I did have extremely realistic nightmares for quite some time. Although I have always had a little fear of the dark, whilst I was using the crystal speculum I did go through a period when I absolutely dreaded the lights being off. Most people can't understand why I have a little fear of the dark even today. I know it is a completely irrational fear, and one which a medium should not have. However, I'm quite certain that it goes a little deeper than that, and that the cultivation of my sensitivity during my early childhood has done quite a lot of emotional and psychological damage. I am trying desperately to find a more gentle way of saying I am definitely not normal!

The Parapsychologist - Ciarán O'Keeffe
Ouija Boards
The Ouija board is a device used to seek out answers to questions

about the past, present and future and to receive messages from ghosts, spirits and other entities in spiritualism. The name is taken from the French *oui* and the German *ja* - both words for 'yes'. The Ouija is thought to be a controversial and dangerous method of interaction with the spirit world. In untrained hands it is believed to attract evil spirits.

Various forms of this method of divination have been used for centuries. In ancient Greece and Rome a small table on wheels was used to point out answers to questions, and I know that in China around 550BC similar devices were being used to communicate with the dead. In 1853 the planchette came into use in Europe. It consisted of a heart-shaped platform on three legs, one of which was a pencil, and the medium would move the device over the paper to spell out messages.

The modern Ouija, which is now marketed as a game, was invented by an American called Elijah J. Bond and sold to William Fuld in 1892, although the names of five other men keep cropping up in the various accounts of its history: Charles Kennard, Harry Rusk, Colonel Washington Bowie, William Maupin, and E.C. Reiche. Reiche was a cabinet-maker, or coffin-maker depending on the source, from Chestertown, Maryland, while Charles Kennard and some of the others are supposedly also connected to the area. Curiously I did my undergraduate degree and embarked on my career in Parapsychology in a small liberal arts college in Chestertown! Fuld founded the Southern Novelty Company in Maryland, which later became the Baltimore Talking Board Company. They called the Ouija board 'Ouija, the Mystifying Oracle'. In 1966 the big toy manufacturers Parker Brothers brought the rights to the board and marketed it so effectively as a game that it sold more than their famous Monopoly game.

The Ouija board itself has a flat smooth surface marked with the letters of the alphabet, the numbers one to ten and the words 'yes' and 'no'. During a séance or other session each participant places a finger on the pointer, or planchette, and asks a question or for a message to be communicated. Although the fingers of the participants are on the planchette there is no conscious control of it and supposedly the planchette spells out the answer under the control of a spirit.

In Parapsychology, the Ouija board is believed to be a form of automatism: an unconscious activity that picks up information from the subconscious mind. Critics say that Ouija boards are dangerous, not only because they can attract evil entities but also because users have no control over repressed material from the subconscious that might be released during a session. Edgar Cayce described it as a 'dangerous toy' and ouija boards have been known to fly out of control as though being directed by some unseen force. Advocates of the ouija board believe it to be a powerful and effective way to make contact with the spirit world, to divine the future and obtain daily guidance.

The ouija board has figured in many cases of mediumship. For example, the entity Seth initiated communication with medium Jane Roberts through a Ouija board in the 1960s and 1970s. And on 8 July1913 a St Louis housewife called Pearl Curran was persuaded by her friend Emily Hutchinson to try the Ouija board. She did so and the name Patience Worth came through. This turned out to be the beginnings of an avalanche of information over a period of five years. Mrs Curran produced 2,500 poems, as lll as short stories, plays and six full-length novels, all allegedly authored by Patience Worth, who claimed to be a seventeenth-century Englishwoman.

Pulitzer Prize winning poet James Merrill used a Ouija board and recorded what he claimed were messages from a number of deceased persons. He combined these messages with his own poetry in *The Changing Light at Sandover*. It's not the only time he's published work based on Ouija messages - in 1976, Merrill published a narrative cycle with a poem for each of the letters A through Z, calling it *The Book of Ephraim*. It was this that formed part of a collection entitled *Divine Comedies* which won the Pulitzer Prize.

The Parker Brothers recommended way of using the board is for two people to sit opposite each other with the board resting on their knees between them. The planchette should be in the centre of the board and the two people should have their fingers lightly resting on it.

One person should act as spokesperson and ask: "Is anybody there?" This should be repeated until the planchette begins to move - hopefully to the yes and then to the centre. It is also possible to work with the board with a number of people sitting around a table, as the more people there are, the more energy is thought to be available to move the planchette. Also just one person can have success working alone with the Ouija board.

The most obvious explanation for how the board works is the conscious, or unconscious, pushing of the planchette. If you've ever participated in a ouija board you may feel as though someone is pushing the planchette. When the participants round the board are asked "Are you pushing it?" there is undoubtedly complete denial. First off, this sort of situation is prone to the psychological principle of group conformity. If you are in a group and one person says one thing and the rest of the group follow suit, it is very difficult for a lone individual to go against what the group says. This was first illustrated by a psychology experiment back in 1951. Asch, the experimenter, asked groups of participants to simply judge which of three lines was the same length as another line (known in psychology as the stimulus line). What the participant didn't realise was that they were in a group with accomplices of the experimenter who were instructed to give the wrong answer. The participant would normally be asked last, or second from last, and 76 per cent of the research participants conformed and gave the answer that was blatantly wrong (but in agreement with the rest of the group). If participants were asked to write down their answer in secret, group conformity disappeared and people gave the right answer. The same sort of thing may happen when a group investigates an allegedly haunted house. If one person hears something and then asks each person in the group whether they did or not, a series of positive responses will only increase pressure on others to conform. The same thing can happen in a Ouija board setting. If you're the last person asked, and you were pushing it, a negative response from everyone else forces you to comply (almost to prevent embarrassment also) and say you weren't either. You then may stop pushing it but the effect could switch to someone else, and so on.

This "influence of suggestion in modifying and directing muscular movement, independently of volition" was given the label 'ideomotor effect' by the psychologist/physiologist William B. Carpenter in 1852. You may not know that you are moving the message indicator, but you are. Proponents of the ideomotor effect generally accept that it is possible to move the planchette unconsciously. They claim that the Ouija board opens a kind of shortcut from the conscious to the subconscious mind. If you're not too scared try doing the Ouija with a blind fold or your eyes closed - get somebody to move the board around so you don't know which way it's orientated. I guarantee the message will be pure gobbledegook! I've conducted many of these experiments before; it relies on the operator being able to see the board and the letters. Penn and Teller demonstrated this wonderfully in their exposé show and simply turned the board 180° when the participants were blindfolded. The planchette kept moving to blank spaces where the participants thought 'Yes' and 'No' should be.

Even as far back as 1919, James Hyslop, in his work entitled 'Contact with another World', discussed the procedural similarities between the Ouija board and automatic writing. He felt that the muscular system of the operators in communication methods such as table-tipping, automatic writing and the Ouija board was the same. He felt there was no mystery in its operation but that the evidence for anything supernatural lay in the actual content rather than the process. Think about it this way - if the messages coming through are mundane, and we can easily attribute them to being part of the operators' conscious or subconscious mind, then surely the most logical explanation is that some muscular movement is actioning the messages (again, either consciously or subconsciously). If the content is completely unknown to the operators and is, in the words of Hyslop, "unmistakably foreign to normal experience", there may be an external source.

Advocates claim that the spirits are making use of the participants' muscles to produce the physical movement. However, it is often difficult to make sense of the communication at first, and words may run into one another or anagrams or codes may be used. In short, although some messages come through loud and clear proponents claim it is often necessary to study messages carefully to make sense of them.

The Ouija board has been condemned by parents and religious groups who say it can cause emotional damage in the impressionable and sometimes even possession. Is this possible? Is the Ouija a potential link to the dark side, where you cannot control what can come through, or is it just a game? Edgar Cayce, the famous American psychic who had a major influence on the modern New Age movement, specifically warned against the use of Ouija, simply stating they were 'dangerous'. Martin Ebon in his book *Satan Trap: Dangers of the Occult*, states:

> *It all may start harmlessly enough, perhaps with a Ouija board. [...] The Ouija will often bring startling information, [...] establishing credibility or identifying itself as someone who is dead. It is common that people who get into this sort of game think of themselves as having been 'chosen' for a special task. [...] Quite often the Ouija turns vulgar, abusive or threatening. It grows demanding and hostile, and sitters may find themselves using the board [...] compulsively, as if 'possessed' by a spirit, or hearing voices that control or command them.*

Most psychics advise against the casual use of the Ouija board, suggesting that it can be a doorway to unknown dimensions or spirits on the lower astral plane who are often very confused and potentially dangerous. This, of course, can't be proved, but if the Ouija does not contact spirits could it access our own subconscious? Possibly, and for this reason if it is to be used for divinatory purposes it should be used with caution.

Despite relentless attempts by sceptics to denounce the Ouija board as merely a game for the suggestible, the negative aspects of this divinatory method are so ingrained in our culture as a result of the media (think of such movies as *The Exorcist!*) that it feels as though it has become the evidence for its own urban legend. There is, therefore, such anticipation and suggestion at work when people sit down to use it or even witness it. I've spoken to hardened cynics who discount all paranormal phenomena as "rubbish" or "easily explained by normal means" but who won't touch a Ouija board. Since there are few accounts of positive, uplifting experiences with the Ouija, and many negative ones, one could assume that it is more associated with the negative aspects of our subconscious, and is therefore best avoided or treated simply as a fun game and nothing more.

The Clairvoyant - Billy Roberts

It is my opinion that even under expert supervision the Ouija board can be dangerous and may also produce some extremely undesirable results. Although it is not fully understood exactly how the Ouija board works, there are innumerable theories as to what produces its phenomena. One Spiritualist theory is that the mental energies of the practitioner somehow interact with the surrounding magnetic field, causing some sort of bio-magnetic force to be created. The more frequently the Ouija board is used, the stronger and more powerfully established the force becomes. After a while it is believed that the bio-magnetic force becomes a conduit for low level astral beings, enabling them to infiltrate the energy field of the practitioner. The mind of the Ouija user is then easily influenced. This continues until a strong, working relationship between the discarnate energy and the Ouija board user is established. Once the discarnate being has obtained the practitioner's confidence, possession is then easily initiated. This theory seems to me to make the most sense. Of course, as a medium I cannot out rule the possibility that the Ouija practitioner is consciously or subconsciously moving the pointer on the Ouija board, only the practitioner can know that.

Another Victorian method of divination was the planchette. This was a simple moveable writing device, in which a pencil was securely fitted. The user would simply sit in a comfortable chair with his or her hand resting gently on the planchette, over a blank piece of paper. A great deal of patience was required before any visible activity was achieved. If successful, the ball-like device would move across the blank piece of paper and begin to write, allegedly in the handwriting of a deceased person. Some practitioners of this sort of paranormal phenomenon did not require a planchette, and would simply sit quietly holding a pencil, until his or her patience paid off, and the hand would move involuntarily, writing in a script that was completely different from the practitioner's own handwriting.

The Clairvoyant - Billy Roberts
Astrology
Astrological Status

I was born on June 24th under the astrological sign of Cancer. According to astrologers that makes me highly emotional, loving and very often insecure. Cancerians are always highly intuitive with a propensity towards being psychic. Over the years I have made a detailed analysis of the astrological signs of mediums, primarily to see if there is a connection between psychic sensitivity and the sign one is born under. My research led me to conclude that certain astrological signs do tend to make extremely good mediums, and that some signs are very communicative and possess a lot of power. The most sensitive signs tend to be those symbolically represented by water, such as Pisces, Scorpio and Cancer. These tend to be the emotional signs and therefore extremely good at touching people's emotions. The fire signs of the Zodiac, Aries, Leo and Sagittarius, are extremely strong, mediumistically speaking, and tend to be quite meticulous of their craft. Often governed by the head, fire signs usually make good trance mediums, particularly Aries, who are usually quite focused and strive relentlessly to develop their abilities.

The Earth signs, Taurus, Virgo and Capricorn, often make good healers. They usually have an extremely practical, down to earth approach to the subject of metaphysics, and are often seen to be very ground. (sense? Better to say "to be very grounded"?) They nearly always produce positive results with Psychometry and tend make an effort to cultivate their craft.

Whilst the air signs, Gemini, Libra and Aquarius nearly always enjoy demonstrating their communication skills, they are often seen to be quite spiritual and always make good mediums and healers. They very often have a strong desire to help other people without seeking any reward.

So, in my opinion the astrological position of your birth certainly does make a great difference to the mediumistic skills you develop, and the degree of sensitivity varies greatly from sign to sign.

Some researchers in the field of mediumship and the cultivation of psychic skills have concluded that mediums are far from being normal, and that there is some sort of abnormality in the way in which a medium's brain functions. I personally have no doubt whatsoever that this is true and I have never felt 'normal', so to speak, particularly when I am working.

The Parapsychologist - Ciarán O'Keeffe
Astrological Status

My birthday is March 21st. Although I'm an Aries, I've been told by a number of astrologers that this means I'm on the cusp. Pisces runs from February 20th to March 20th and Aries from March 21st to April 20th. There are numerous publications stating that there are particular personality traits I should have being an Aries. Other astrologers I've spoken to have corrected this misconception of the 'cusp'. So, for example, the astrologer David Wells has looked at my natal chart and says I am definitely an Aries (00 28 degrees to be precise) and that being born on the cusp refers to the Sun cutting perfectly through the cusp (start point) of a new astrological house in a natal chart. In other words "is the sun in the 4th or 5th house for example; will you be housewife of the year or social climber of the decade?"

I don't have any belief in astrology but, despite a distinct lack of scientific support for it, astrology is embedded in contemporary society. The discipline of *horary* astrology (or popular astrology) has been popularized by mass-circulation newspapers. These 'horoscopes' offer day-to-day advice based solely on a person's astrological sign (otherwise known as the 'star' or 'zodiac sign', e.g. Aries, Libra, Capricorn, etc). *Genethliacal* astrologers, on the other hand, construct and interpret personalized, lifeline horoscopes known as 'birth charts' (or 'natal charts'). Estimates of an individual's destiny are computed on the basis of longitude, latitude, and precise time of birth. Most astrologers are contemptuous of the sun-sign approach, maintaining that accurate details of birth date, location and time are necessary for a precise horoscope. However, scientific studies have examined the accuracy of both horary and genethliacal astrology.

Newspaper Horoscopes *(Horary Astrology)*

Many studies frequently quote statistics on the popularity and belief in astrology as adequate reasoning for assessment of the claimants. Yet the majority of survey statistics are based on the public's reaction to, and interest in, newspaper horoscopes (*horary* astrology), whilst the majority of astrology studies focus on the creation and manipulation of natal charts (*genethliacal* astrology). Explanation and study of such newspaper horoscopes is limited to work on the Barnum effect whilst few researchers have posited other explanations for the acceptance of horoscopes.

Some researchers have explored how 'membership group saliency' may account for the success of newspaper horoscopes. According to this theory "the imposition of a membership group does have some effect on an individual's attitudes, even when the imposed group is not accepted by the individual as his reference group". Think of it like in-group/out-group, or supporting a football team. If you support Capricorn, for example, you're not likely to be interested in Libra or Taurus. Some researchers, including myself, have tested this 'group' idea that the presence of a zodiac 'label' (e.g. Aries, Cancer, Capricorn, etc) would result in the general public applying more relevance to it than otherwise.

Personality traits and sun-signs

Various studies have examined the relationship between sun-signs and various personality tests. The earliest such experiments employed the California Personality Inventory (CPI) did find a slight relationship between the CPI femininity index and season of birth. Later work, however, found no relationship between sun-sign and personality. Positive findings were not replicated in two later studies. Many studies focused on an extroversion/introversion difference (often associated with 'active' and 'passive' signs, respectively) as determined by the Eysenck Personality Inventory (EPI). Two studies found a relationship between astrological factors and the Introversion/Extroversion index of the Eysenck Personality Inventory, though later replications found no additional support for these findings. Other studies compiled natal charts and the results of the Minnesota Multiphasic Personality Inventory (MMPI); the Cattell 16 PF Personality Inventory; the Leary Interpersonal Checklist and found no relationships.

Birth Chart Horoscopes (*Genethliacal Astrology*)

There have been scientific studies that have attempted to test the validity of astrology by examining the potential relationship between an individual's personality and the configurations of the constellations and planets within the zodiac (i.e. an area of the sky 16° wide that extends around the earth roughly parallel to the equator). One researcher took two samples of 1586 and 1392 marriages from Michigan from the years 1967-1968. He found no support for compatible relationships as dictated by astrology (tested using marriage-divorce statistics). Others have focused on personality types prevalent in certain professions: politicians; athletes, actors, scientists and writers; and various other occupations; including even murderers. In all studies, no relationship was found with sun-signs or zodiac signs containing certain planets that are associated with particular career traits (e.g. *Mars* indicates courage and aggression, an expected correlate with a career in the army). Only one study, examining the link between the 'iron-willed' temperament of elite sportsmen and the presence of Mars in their charts' critical zones, resulted in significant findings (the famous Gauquelin astrology study). The findings of this work on astrology have prompted a long and complex debate. A recent re-analysis of the Gauquelin data found evidence for hitherto unsuspected social artefacts. The majority of work in this area, however, has primarily focused on statistical analyses of sets of birthdates and their corresponding planetary configurations in an attempt to verify, at least in principle, the validity of horoscope analysis. Without access to exact birth times (i.e. time of day the birth occurred), and therefore omitting valuable information, astrologers would be reluctant to construct and interpret a natal chart. In one day, for example, the ascendant position can be found at "any point along the zodiac, depending on the relative orientation of the horizon and the ecliptic".

Chapter 10
Meditation

The Clairvoyant - Billy Roberts

My first experience with meditation took place sometime around 1966. Transcendental meditation was just becoming quite popular, primarily as a result of The Beatles, who had become devotees of the guru and innovator of T.M, as it was known. T.M's creator was Indian physicist, the Maharishi Mahesh Yogi, who had westernized a yogic method of meditation, claiming that it would release stress and encourage a more focused and relaxed mind, ultimately encouraging the state of 'Nirvana'. In other words, meditation was exactly what westerners needed to free them from the shackles of modern day living. However, Transcendental meditation apparently caused psychological and emotional in some practitioners, causing them to be unbalanced rather than balanced. My interest in T.M developed when I was working as a professional musician and living in France. At first I just got involved with T.M simply because it was fashionable to do so. After a while, though, I began having very strange experiences during meditation. Some of these experiences were quite pleasant and some were not. My interest in the whole process of meditation and exactly what it could produce in me deepened. The only problems I had with Transcendental meditation was with the method itself. It did not really suit me, and so I decided to modify the method I used until I felt comfortable with it. Although I still used a mantra, I combined this with the use of a Yantra, a geometric shape or design. In fact, I used this method for many years, and today teach it to others in my workshops and seminars. Although this process is an extremely effective meditation technique, it is also very powerful, which is why T.M was viewed by the church with some disdain and great apprehension. I am wondering what a psychologist would have to say about this sort of meditation, and whether it would be regarded with cynicism and disdain, in the same way that mediumship is regarded by the church and by science? After all, the results of meditation are esoteric and totally subjective, exactly in the same way as the whole process of mediumship. Meditation is a means of accessing higher states of consciousness, in the same way that mediumship allows the medium's mind to access higher and more subtle states of awareness. Although the results are slightly different, the methods are exactly the same. What does my friend Ciarán have to say about that!

The Parapsychologist - Ciarán O'Keeffe

Despite an outward appearance of a scientist hardened and immediately defensive to any New Age or esoteric claims I am willing to listen to claims and also attempt to experience them. It is for this reason that, aside from the thousands of hours of reading and research, I have spent considerable time experiencing firsthand things like hypnotherapy (12 weeks of hypnotherapy sessions), massage and Reiki (studied at a London 'school'), rune casting, aromatherapy, Chi Kung, and meditation. Admittedly it was a brief sojourn into the world of meditation but whilst studying for my Masters I took evening meditation classes at a Yoga centre in Liverpool. The experience was certainly relaxing and calming although I am generally a calm person anyway. The technique of being able to focus, whilst at the same time freeing the mind of the usual everyday stresses, worries and general clutter, was a valuable one. The claim of various schools of meditation in reaching higher levels of consciousness is a tricky one. It's not tricky because I'm wearing my sceptical hat again; it's because of the word 'consciousness'. What is consciousness? This is one of the most difficult questions to answer or, perhaps I should say, to put into words. Everyone has their own personal understanding of what it is. So to argue that meditation can help reach higher levels of consciousness is open to individual interpretation. There is no way I could have reached the sort of levels I've been told about in my short time practising yogic meditation (at least that's what I've been told), but there were moments of deep serenity, calm, and inner focus. Were those moments of higher levels of consciousness? If that sounds a little bit too 'New Agey' for me, it is. Listening to other members of the group wax lyrical about "higher transcendental dimensions and chakras opening" and others succumb to group conformity and feel the need to report anything spiritual just so they didn't look left out became a little too much for me. I remember earlier on in the meditation sessions reporting nothing, just describing my image of a candle flame and the worries about the day's events. Some of the looks I got from group members were enough to freeze you to the spot!

There are other claims of meditation, though they are restricted to certain schools of thought. For example, there is the claim made by Transcendental Meditation that you can gain the ability to levitate or fly. I think there is less said about it nowadays and you rarely hear the claim made but in the past it resulted in TM receiving a lot of publicity. Well, it received a lot of publicity until some televised public demonstrations of the levitating showed it to be little more than yogic 'hopping'. Those meditating would sit cross-legged in the traditional position and after sometime would start hopping across mats on the floor.

The only real problem I have with meditation is the money making behind it. Sure evening classes have to charge, and teachers need money to cover their time, guides recommending different approaches are all necessary I suppose but when you hear of people being charged for mantras or leaders of certain schools wallowing in wealth (I believe the Maharishi Mahesh Yogi's business was worth over $3 billion in the late 1990s), it makes you question the underlying motivation. This is especially the case when meditation appears to be such a personal (transpersonal) experience and is an elementary process to start with. It then simply requires motivation, focus, time and determination to reach higher levels, whatever they may be.

Chapter 11
Superstition

The Clairvoyant - Billy Roberts
From a very early age most of us have grown up with the beliefs and superstitions passed on to us by our parents. And even though we secretly know these to be just ill-informed nonsense, they are so deeply embedded in our subconscious that we dare not disregard them for fear that something dreadful will befall us. Even today I simply will not walk under a ladder, just in case it brings me bad luck, or something terrible happens to me. Even though I have no idea where this belief came from, I will not, and cannot, take the chance. My mother would not do it, so I most certainly will not!

However, some omens and superstitions do make a great deal of sense and clearly do have more than a grain of truth in them. For example, I grew up believing that you should never cut your toenails on a Sunday. This, I am quite convinced, was a superstition created by my mother in order to stop my father from performing such an unpleasant practice in the living room, just before Sunday lunch was served. Another superstition passed on from my mother was to never play cards on a Sunday. Doing so, my mother assured me, would result in the devil playing along with us.

Other beliefs are so ridiculous that they are obviously designed to instil fear into the vulnerable and gullible. For example - never cross another person on the stairs! In the house where I lived as a child, this was not only ridiculous, but also an impossibility, for the stairs were so narrow that there was only enough room for one person at a time.

"See a pin, pick it up, and all the day you'll have good luck!" How ridiculous! My mother collected so many pins that there was very little room in her purse for any money.

I remember watching an elderly woman at the bus stop knowingly allowing her bus to go on without her, because she had dropped her glove on the pavement and wanted someone to pick it up for her.

Although I could never understand my mother saying, "A knife to the floor and a man to the door," she always seemed to be right. Every time she dropped a knife on the floor, a man would call at the house for one reason or another.

Some superstitions never really made any sense to me, and I could never see why crossed knives were unlucky. They do say that the crossed knives superstition originated with the crossed swords in a duel. The belief is that when knives cross on the table an argument ensues.

Another superstition is to never place new shoes on a table or flat surface. This portends a long period of bad luck, and in the grimmest scenario, DEATH! The origins of this morbid superstition originate with thirteen wooden steps up to the gallows. It is thought that anyone who places new shows on a flat surface brings bad luck to the household or even worse.

As a child I used to laugh with delight as my father threw a pinch of salt over his left shoulder after spilling it on the table. This ancient superstition of spilling salt necessitated throwing the salt as an offering to the spirits. Even he was superstitious about some things.

I remember when my grandmother died and her coffin had been placed on trestles in the parlour, all the mirrors in the house were covered with a black cloth. This was to ensure that my grandmother's reflection could not be seen in the mirror.

Then there was the time I got smacked for accidentally breaking a mirror. "We'll have bad luck for seven years now!" my mother said, with a worried look upon her face. Apparently, bad luck only follows a broken mirror if it is broken on purpose. That's all right then!

In some way, the superstition of touching wood to protect you when you have tempted fate has a biblical origin. The followers of Jesus touched the wood of the cross as a mark of respect. Knocking on wood is also supposed to scare off evil spirits. Crossing fingers also has Christian connotations. Long before the cross was a Christian symbol of recognition, a drawing of a fish was used. Crossed fingers designated the fish and were used as a secret sign to let others know you were a follower of Jesus.

One of the most ridiculous superstitions originated in the trenches in the First World War when a soldier was shot dead after taking the third light for his cigarette. I wonder what would have happened if he had been shot dead after the first one? Smoking would have then been a thing of the past.

I have always found the black cat superstition quite fascinating. For example, Winston Churchill was born on Friday 13th, and he would never pass a black cat without stroking it. Napoleon, however, had a dread of black cats. If he saw one he believed that bad luck would befall him. Some people believe that it is lucky for a black cat to cross your path, whilst others believe the opposite. All black cat superstitions are believed to originate from the fact that witches had their black familiars - the wise cats that always accompanied them.

Another silly superstition is about tripping on the stairs. Tripping up the stairs is said to mean a birth, tripping down the stairs portends death. This is one of those little known superstitions, but I suppose that now you know about it, many of you will take care not to do it - at least not to trip on your way down.

Then we have those portentous omens that are usually associated with death. Knocking sounds from within a cupboard, or ottoman, is one example of a portent of death. Clocks suddenly stopping, or falling off a wall or mantelpiece, and a mirror or picture suddenly falling from the wall are viewed similarly. A dog howling was nearly always considered to be an omen of misfortune or approaching bad news. When anyone dies a dog always howls. Have you ever noticed this?

The reflection of a new moon in a mirror would always necessitate the turning of silver coins in the pocket. Do this, and you would be guaranteed good fortune, ignore the omen, and misfortune would most certainly befall you. I could never understand why a purse could not be given as a gift without first of all placing a coin inside it. Or why a knife of any sort had to be accompanied by a coin before being given as a present. It would appear that, like dialects which are peculiar to certain geographical locations, superstitions too vary somewhat from place to place.

As a child I would suddenly get it into my head that I could not walk on the cracks on the pavement. If I managed to follow my route all the way home without treading on any cracks, I was convinced that I would become a millionaire. I am not sure what happened, perhaps I walked on a crack without realizing it!

I am quite certain that some superstitions are created by children who often possess the power to turn a simple phrase into a powerful incantation. "Touch black, no back," would have to be intoned to ensure that a transaction between playmates was fixed and the comics or toys could not be taken back after they had been swapped. As a child we would also have to put up with the annoying ritual of having our head touched and 'first wet', called every time we had visited the barber.

Putting two different socks on by mistake was also meant to herald the approach of a lucky period, and wearing an item of clothing inside out was also supposed to be extremely lucky. If my mother inadvertently changed the month on a calendar before it was due, she would be certain that something untoward was going to happen to her. If a wild bird flew into the house, my mother would be adamant that someone was going to die, and if a gypsy woman called to the door, she would not send her away without purchasing a lucky charm, just in case she cursed her.

I suppose the majority of people from my mother's era were superstitious, and today the tradition has largely disappeared. Perhaps that is the problem in the so-called modern age of science and technology; there is only a small minority who have retained the tradition of adhering to superstitions. However, the majority of people "touch wood" when tempting fate and "never cast a clout till May is out!"

When walking along the pavement with your friend or partner, never let a lamp post or any other obstacle come between you. If you do your relationship will be broken.

When a question needs to be resolved and an answer is sought, a tossed coin frequently makes the decision. Some people feel that they have to wear a certain lucky tie, or even carry a particular lucky charm when going for an interview or into a situation in which extra luck is required.

Whenever I am going into a stressful situation, or perhaps appearing somewhere quite important, I always carry a photograph of Padre Pio. I also have to wear a certain pair of socks. Some people carry superstitions to the extreme and become obsessed to the point where it prevents them from doing something important. One man believed that rain was unlucky for him, and so missed an important interview because it was raining.

Triskaidekaphobia

What about the superstition about the number thirteen? Some people unfortunately career their phobia and superstition of Friday the 13th to the extreme. Triskaidekaphobia is the irrational fear of Friday the 13th - a morbid dread that even prevents the sufferer from actually doing anything at all on that day. In fact, the number 13 has been a deeply ingrained symbol of bad luck in many countries for centuries. Although in China and Japan the number 13 has no particular significance - 4 is unlucky, perhaps because the Chinese character or ideograph for 4 also signifies death. 1 and 3 equals 4: the fourth month of the year is April. 13th April is probably the unluckiest Friday the 13th on the calendar. It is a known fact that statistically more people have accidents on Friday 13th than any other day of the year; in fact, statistically there are known to be more admissions to hospital on this day also.

It is believed to be unlucky to seat 13 people at a table, most probably because of the 13 people seated at the Last Supper. In fact, Jesus is said to have predicted that one of them would betray him. In ancient Babylon, 13 people were chosen to personify the god in a religious ceremony. However, one person was always seated away from the others, and he or she was the one chosen to be sacrificed. It is said that if there are 13 letters in your name you are cursed with the luck of the devil. Charles Manson, Theodore Bundy to name but two infamous characters with thirteen letters in their names. Many people believe that if 13 people sit down to dinner, they will all die within one year. The ancient Hindus and Vikings believed that it was unlucky for 13 people to gather in one place. In fact, number thirteen is very rarely seen in any street, and the thirteenth floor in any tall building is very often referred to as either the 113th floor, or the 14th floor. The number 13 is often associated with death, misfortune or even the devil.

Fear of anything is probably one of the most destructive forces, and if allowed to persist, will eventually precipitate the power of 'attraction', thereby causing whatever it is that is feared to actually happen. If allowed to persist, superstition can quite easily become a phobia; and anything you fear is automatically empowered. In the United States some people won't even go to work on Friday 13th; some won't eat in restaurants; many would not think of setting a wedding date. I would be quite interest to know what you (Ciarán) have to say about superstitions and if they have any real bearing on reality? Or are superstitions just integral parts of Pagan folklore that have persisted through the ages? More importantly, how do you think superstitions affect our lives, psychologically speaking?

The Parapsychologist - Ciarán O'Keeffe

I'm not superstitious. Before I give my view on the whole matter, I encourage all of you who have any slight inclination towards superstitious behaviour to pick up, now, a copy of Stuart Vyse's book entitled *Believing in Magic: The Psychology of Superstition*. I have never been superstitious though I have early recollections of my Mum encouraging me to touch wood if anything bad was said. I quickly reduced this behaviour to a joke by touching my head one day in response to the instruction. Since then it has been a fascination of mine to witness people's lives dictated by superstition. I marvel at friends and colleagues counting magpies, avoiding ladders, cowering at black cats and screaming at broken mirrors when all that's happening is a false conception of causation, a particular form of irrational behaviour.

For me, superstition is a way of thinking about the world that ensures we have a handle on the unknown or uncertain. A perfect illustration of this comes from an anthropologist, Bronislaw Malinowski, who spent four years, in 1914, living amongst the Trobriand islanders, off the coast of New Guinea. There he found that scientific knowledge and magical thinking existed side by side. The Trobrianders who fished in calm lagoon waters used standardized and tested methods of catching. Alternatively, the islanders who sailed out to open sea and fished in unsafe, unpredictable waters performed detailed magical rituals to make certain they returned safely with a healthy catch.

It can also be used in less dramatic contexts. Consider, for example, the gambler sitting at a roulette wheel habitually crossing his fingers or rubbing a talisman. It is not a dangerous situation like the fishing scenario described above (unless he's gambling all his money, house, car, job, wife, kids, dog etc., on where the ball stops). In fact the gambler is probably aware that there's a chance he may not win. So why is he indulging in superstitious behaviour? It is still another case of someone trying to get a handle on the unknown. The outcome is unknown but if he can somehow steer the outcome in his favour, all the better. By using a talisman or having a superstitious ritual he feels he is increasing his chances. If he does win then it merely reinforces the superstitious behaviour and if he has no knowledge of how random occurrences work or how to judge probability and coincidence then it adds to a reliance on superstitious rituals. Let's take a simple example – if you throw a die and are betting on 2, 4, or 6 coming up, what are the chances you'll win? You've got a 50/50 chance of winning. The same as betting on 'heads' landing face up when you flip a coin. Assuming it is a fair die, or a fair coin (i.e. not fixed), with each throw the chances never change. Yet a misunderstanding of probability would lead people to believe that if there had been a run of 6s then on the next throw a 6 is least likely. The same way that if you had a run of 'heads' you would expect 'tails' to appear on the next throw, though 'heads' is equally likely (in a manner of speaking). A gambler betting on even numbers turning up on a die, who is using a superstitious habit, could possibly attribute a reoccurring 6 to his actions rather than simple probability.

Probability & the Paranormal

A few years ago I looked at this concept of probability judgement with my wife. Since she is also an academic psychologist (specialising in probability and decision making) we both got a kick out of combining our mutual interests into one study: probability and the paranormal. There is the often quoted idea that believers in the paranormal, and also perhaps superstitious people, are less accurate in probability judgement than non-believers. In a book from 2001 entitled *Parapsychology: The Science of Unusual Experience*, in which various parapsychologists contribute chapters on their areas of speciality, two authors even go so far as to state "specifically, the believers are more likely to underestimate the probability of a chance event...Believers may thus tend to misperceive chance events as being beyond coincidence." But where does the evidence for this come from? Simple answer, there is none. People are generally poor at probability judgements, regardless of their belief.

Back in the 1980s the renowned sceptic, Susan Blackmore, proposed that belief in the paranormal (and hence superstition) could be explained by a sort of misjudgement whereby some individuals tend to consistently underestimate the chances that coincidences will occur (e.g. a prophetic dream of an accident). This idea was extrapolated from the work of Kahneman and Tversky who said that probability judgements, generally, are notoriously inaccurate. According to Blackmore's idea, such low subjective probabilities lead believers to seek paranormal-type explanations when confronted with coincidental events, thus reinforcing their belief. She presented volunteers with a number of problems (four) that entailed assessing probabilities. One of the problems was the classic "Birthday Paradox". The Birthday Paradox goes like this – How many people would you have to have in a room for there to be a 50/50 chance that 2 of them share exactly the same birthday?

Her study showed that there was a difference between believers and non-believers but on only one of the probability problems, the Birthday paradox. This result, however, failed to replicate in a later study by Susan Blackmore and a colleague who was an applied mathematician. Two other psychologists, in 1999, presented participants with the same problems among other probabilistic tasks. They found no link between probabilistic reasoning scores and degree of belief. Susan Blackmore, herself, even stated in 1994 following a newspaper survey, that "The probability misjudgement hypothesis suggests that sheep [believers] should generally be worse at estimating probabilities than goats [non-believers]...this was not found and the difference scores are remarkably similar for sheep and goats." Despite this, over 20 years after Susan Blackmore's original study, the argument about probability and paranormal belief is still put forward by cynics. Do you know the answer to the Birthday Paradox? Whether you believe in the paranormal or not, are superstitious or not, you'd still be surprised by the answer. 23

As a little postscript to this chapter, I just have to clarify one fascinating fact that Billy has raised. Triskaidekaphobia is actually fear of the number 13, or more specifically fear of things associated with the number 13. Although a phobia of Friday 13th does come under this remit, the actual term for a morbid fear of that particular day is either friggatriskaidekaphobia (frigga referring to an ancient Scandinanvian fertility and love goddess who was worshipped on a Friday) or paraske-videkatriaphobia (a term coined by the fear specialist Dr. Dossey who claims that if you can pronounce the word you are cured - I've yet to see the evidence though)!

Chapter 12
Spiritual Healing

The Clairvoyant - Billy Roberts

What seems like a lifetime away now, I received regular Spiritual Healing from a gentleman by the name of Desmond Tierney. It was he who helped me through an extremely difficult time, and for that I would always be grateful to him. After him I had healing from Helen Yaffe, a lady for whom I had the greatest of respect. She too was an excellent healer, and even had a regular clinic in the neurological unit of Walton Hospital in Liverpool. It was as a direct result of these two people that I became very interested in the whole process of healing, until eventually, I too became a healer member of the National Federation of Spiritual Healers, one of the largest healing organizations in the world. However, sometime in the early 90s I began to analyse the whole process of healing and, as a result, began to feel a little uncomfortable with the actual administration of healing. Like the majority of healers practising under the auspices of the National Federation, people seeking healing would contact me after receiving several names of healers on the NFSH list. Although a minority of those seeking healing were suffering with fairly minor conditions that frequently responded well to healing, the majority were seeking healing as a 'last result', when conventional medicine had failed and the prognosis bleak. Although I personally know that healing does help on both a psychological as well as a spiritual level, I can honestly say that I have never seen healing cure cancer completely, even though there are many who will vehemently affirm that healing cured them of an incurable cancerous condition. Therefore, the problem I have with 'spiritual healing' is whether or not many healers (myself included,) are merely deluding themselves, and the healing process itself is no more than an exercise in psychological and emotional reassurance. Although there is obviously an exchange of 'something' during the healing process, I would like to ask you (Ciarán) what you believe this is and what you think takes place when healing is given to a sick person?

The Parapsychologist - Ciarán O'Keeffe

I have to admit spiritual healing is not an area of expertise for me. By that I mean I haven't researched it extensively as part of my studies, or witnessed it, or heard many accounts about it or even been subject to it at any point in my life. My only real exposure to it has been reading two books by Harry Edwards, briefly experimenting with Reiki, and also looking, in detail, into distant healing by prayer. Some would argue, though, that Harry Edwards' writings on the topic are a very good place to start. I'm admitting this because it's right for readers to know that I'm only offering opinion based on some research I've done for this book, as opposed to other 'paranormal' topics covered thus far that are more my area of expertise. My first, instinctive reaction to the topic, is that we're largely dealing with the 'Placebo Effect'. Even the little academic reading I've done on the topic reveals that there is no scientific evidence for 'spiritual healing' working. By that I mean there are no peer reviewed replicated scientific studies proving that spiritual healing works. Out there, once you start to look, there are flashes of fascinating debates and studies that put forward very convincing arguments (for example, Serena Roney-Dougal's ongoing research). Before you jump out of your hospital bed, however, or run out of the GP's waiting room, I'd like you to make an informed decision.

Let's clarify what spiritual healing actually is - for me it covers, as addressed by the NFSH, the use of alleged energy in the healing process where the only source of that energy is spiritual. Does that sound vague? Sorry, it is. It has to be an all-encapsulating definition because, from my perspective, it does cover many different styles. It includes the stereotypical laying on of hands that many may be familiar with, or the simple request that Spirit provide the healing, or the healer allowing the state of trance control to guide the process, etc. Regardless of the mode of spiritual healing, the interaction and anecdotal success of it relies on two things. The first concerns spontaneous remission. The medical profession is aware that even for the most severe ailments there are a small percentage of patients who recover without explanation. Some medical practitioners attribute such recovery to normal influences that were unobservable (e.g. diet or work change, weather conditions etc) misdiagnosis and there are other cases where it is fraud perpetuated to market a new 'miracle cure'. The majority of evidence for spontaneous remission, however, is anecdotal but there's no denying the fact that the term exists in medicine (pick up a medical dictionary) and there are accurate cases fully reported by physicians throughout history. There is strong evidence to suggest that the body's natural immune system could be responsible for recovery. No matter what the reason is for it happening, even this perfectly natural explanation for spiritual healing remains a bit of a mystery. If spontaneous remission is not the answer, perhaps a related effect, the placebo, is.

Placebo is Latin for "I shall please." The placebo effect is when medicine, or a medical treatment, that is totally harmless and innocuous is administered to a patient and the patient recovers. It has been observed for a small percentage of people in controlled medical studies and, I would argue, is also observed with the majority of alternative therapies. The reason I say this is because it relies on the power of suggestion and therefore only works because of the belief of the patient. The patient has to believe the medicine is going to work for it to have any effect. This belief in the effectiveness of the treatment can come from prior beliefs on the method (for example, homeopathy) or can occur simply as a result of the interaction with the practitioner. For example, if the practitioner in front of you exudes confidence and appeals to your reason by appearing qualified and knowledgeable then you are more likely to trust them and believe in the effectiveness of the treatment. Additionally, if this is the 'last ditch effort' in your attempt to cure a persistent illness, you are more likely to believe in it working. All of these scenarios aid in the power of suggestion, the placebo effect and ultimately, your recovery. Remember, though, that even if all of the above conditions are right, it may not work. So, if that's the case, why does the placebo effect happen? Surely if that's what is going on with spiritual healing that means, it works, no?

The placebo effect happens because of a number of possible reasons. Firstly, as mentioned before, a patient's beliefs, hopes and suggestibility could be responsible which ultimately guide the body's immune system into action. Secondly it could work because a proportion of feeling ill is role-playing. I don't mean we act ill, I mean that when you get a cold there are certain behaviours that, socially and culturally, you are meant to manifest - sniffling, tiredness, dreariness, etc. If this is the case then a placebo works because you are role-playing, you 'role-play' the recovery. Thirdly, it could be because of spontaneous remission. Note, a cold could go away without taking medicine. Also, because of the level of belief the placebo may actually 'trick' the brain, which could evoke a healing response based on previous experience. Fourthly, the intense interpersonal communication of the practitioner, the touching and focused attention, could all result in mood changes which could, in turn, result in physical changes. Changes in mood and emotion do have a physical consequence (i.e. endorphin release). In addition any reduction in stress, anxiety or depression caused by the illness ensures no further complications and these things are easily reduced in a healing environment. Think of an alternative therapy centre where aromatherapy, calming music and caring staff greet you as you enter. Imagine, on the one hand, that a slightly depressed person with a sore throat is left in a waiting room at the local GP where the room is painted white, is noisy and there are other ill people around and is then either palmed off with a prescription or told to go home and get some sleep. On the other hand, another person with the same symptoms visits a spiritual healer. Which, do you think, would recover first?

This may all appear to be a sceptical argument that, in some way supports spiritual healing. A word of warning, however, as placebos have shown only limited success with only a limited number and type of illnesses (e.g. pain, headaches, depression, stomach complaints such as ulcer, etc). Those wishing for an immediate solution to their illness, however, should be aware that placebos may not offer an immediate cure, whereas many non-placebo medicines and treatment do. Also, only about 30 per cent of people appear to be susceptible to placebo effects, and it is useless without being able to predict whether a person is or not. Additionally, and this is perhaps where the main ethical issues with spiritual healing and some alternative therapies lie, placebo effects are not long term and so any debilitating disease or chronic health problem could return. So, counter to previous chapters where Billy and I came up with topic areas and then wrote our thoughts on them, I began this section by essentially responding to Billy's questions. I hope I've answered them and I think there are some aspects with which we are in agreement. In terms of whether there is an "exchange of 'something'" in the healing process, as Billy puts it. Yes, I think there is, an exchange of false hope.

I'd like to finish with a little funny anecdote about my interaction with a renowned healer. I was conducting studies on psychics as part of my Masters thesis on psychic criminology. I had recruited a number of renowned UK psychics as well as local (North West) based psychics. One of them was a renowned healer, as well as claiming she had worked with the police. We got on famously and she had a fabulous sense of humour. She, let's call her Mary, was due to come into the lab on a particular day and never showed. I had a senior police officer standing by, objects from crime scenes, the lab booked etc. I called her and this is my recollection of part of the phone conversation:

Me: "Mary, how come you didn't call or show up today?"
Mary: "I'm sorry Ciarán, I've been ill, a nasty flu."
Me: "But Mary, if you're such an amazing healer why did you get ill?"
Mary: "Oh, Ciarán. I give out so much love and healing there's never any left for me!"

Chapter 13
The Clairvoyant &
The Parapsychologist

Final Questions, Final Thoughts
The Clairvoyant questions The Parapsychologist -
Billy asks Ciarán

Do you have a genuine interest in the paranormal, or is it a purely commercial one?
Ciarán answers: I have a genuine interest in the paranormal; I hope this book has evidenced that. If the paranormal was a purely commercial venture then "I'm in the wrong and on the wrong side of the fence." That is a better question asked to particular people in the paranormal community who make the most money: certain mediums; psychics; angel therapists; aura readers; healers etc.

As a parapsychologist, would you have any objection if any of your children showed signs of being psychic? If the latter did happen, would you encourage him/her to develop their skills further, or would you apply your skills as a psychologist to 'cure' the problem?
Ciarán answers: What a great question! This is aside from the questionable nature of psychic ability and aside from me and my wife testing the child under controlled conditions and the results being positive, and replicated in a different lab and with different experimenters? (Just kidding!) I wouldn't object, no. I'd hope that they could grow up, though, learning all possible explanations from us for their ability and ultimately making their own decision. Isn't it the same sort of question which could be directed at parents who hate football and their child wanted to be a footballer? In other words, as a responsible parent I'd want my child to be happy and would encourage

them in whatever endeavour they chose.

If all religions were removed from the world, and all notions of an after-life along with any unusual paranormal skills were deleted from our memories, in your opinion as a psychologist how do you think this would affect us?
Ciarán answers: Phew! A tough one. I think the removal of any notions of an after-life or any ingrained, instinctual hope of an afterlife, could take the world in either of two directions. On the one hand it could become a miserable place as many people with unfortunate lives will realize that there is nothing better later on. On the other hand, people will know that this is there only chance, they have only one life, and so will really make a go of it. There would be no apathy, laziness, perhaps no wars. Additionally there'd be less chance of wars because many wars have had a religious underpinning. Without a concept of the afterlife it is difficult to imagine religions. In fact, I seem to be talking myself round to the frequently proffered idea that religion and belief in the paranormal are an innately human trait that exists because of our make up, our brain hard wiring, or because of our socialisation and culture and the way we see the world.

Looking at the worse case morbid scenario: you have reached the end of your life; achieved everything you have wanted to achieve in life, but now you are faced with your own mortality and are going to die - do you believe or just hope that there is something beyond death?
Ciarán answers: If I'm on my deathbed the only thing I'd be thinking about with regards to the afterlife would be "Now I'll know."

Have you ever had a private consultation with a medium? If you have, how did you rate it?
Ciarán answers: I've had many readings from mediums though they haven't been in the traditional context. I've had unsolicited readings from mediums who have taken part in my experiments and others who

I've met as part of my research, who have just given snippets of information and I've had a number of readings from Spiritualist Mediums whilst attending Spiritualist Church (whilst doing my PhD). In any of these contexts I didn't get readings that I was impressed with or that I didn't have an alternative explanation for. I'll be honest and say that since completing my undergraduate degree I was probably the worst person to give a reading for due to my sceptical nature. Sometimes I was constantly aware of alternative explanations regarding cold reading etc and so would purposely not give anything away, even remaining quiet when questioned. Other times I was equally aware but didn't want to make the situation more difficult for the medium and so would be overly eager to please, often nodding just out of encouragement.

What do you think of the theory that Schizophrenia is a low-grade form of mediumship?

Ciarán answers: I'm not sure where this theory comes from and I suspect it originates more with paranormal believers (can I say your side?) than sceptics or parapsychologists. The reason I say this is because parapsychologists, on the whole, have a psychology background and are trained, at university level, and have knowledge in most areas of psychology. Therefore they'd know about schizophrenia and would probably answer 'no'. This is because there are three major subtypes of schizophrenia - Catatonic, Paranoid and Disorganized - each with particular characteristics, none of which (aside from auditory hallucinations) match the sort of behaviour you get from the majority of mediums. Catatonic schizophrenics are either, as the name suggests, catatonic, or extremely hyperactive. Paranoid schizophrenics are the type that most people are aware of. They suffer from paranoid or grandiose delusions. Disorganized schizophrenics manifest "disturbed behaviour which appears strange or inappropriate to the situation they are in, and they are often extremely socially withdrawn" (Hayes, 2000). The main point that you're making, I think, is that particular schizophrenics suffer from auditory hallucinations and that this may be linked to mediumship. The problem is, however, that according to the diagnostic manual that is used by professionals a person has to display two or more symptoms to be diagnosed with schizophrenia. Only one is concerned with auditory hallucinations. There are, though I'm not a psychiatrist specializing in this disorder, circumstances where someone can be diagnosed with schizophrenia if they only report hallucinations. The auditory hallucinations would have to be, however, a running commentary from a single voice or a perpetual conversation between two or more voices. I had one of my MSc students conduct a qualitative study on this examining the reports of voices from schizophrenics and those from mediums. The difference in content, style and frequency is enormous. For this reason, and because other symptoms aren't found in any mediums I've met, I'd have to say no. The over-riding reason for saying no, though, is the attempt to link a mental health disorder with mediumship. No matter which side you start from it just doesn't seem to sit right.

What would you do if, as a result of your head sustaining a minor injury, you suddenly began to 'see' so-called dead people?
Ciarán answers: I'd hope that I retained some element of rationality in my brain to be aware of the injury and put it forward as a possible explanation for my second sight. If it's merely seeing random dead people without any semblance of evidence then it would be easier for someone like me to explain away as visual hallucinations. If I started to actually see dead people and they appeared at appropriate moments next to living people and started to provide 'evidence' of their presence then the first place I'd go would be to a colleague in Parapsychology and I'd asked to be tested. If it's proven under those conditions then I might use the ability to expose charlatans. Beyond that I'm not sure. I might visit murderers who hadn't been caught but whose victims had appeared (with surveillance equipment and back-up). I might write a book...

I personally believe that we met solely to write this and other projects: what is your opinion? (Sorry, a difficult one.)
Ciarán answers: The implication with this question is that there's some sort of fate or synchronicity involved. If that's the case then it's not the same belief as me. I don't 'believe' in synchronicity or that things happen for a reason. There are hundreds of thousands of possible paths our lives could take from any particular point in time which could lead us to thousands of possible outcomes, any of which could be fabulous or awful or appear to be as a result of some sort of destiny. It's a chaotic world we live in and sometimes we make the choices that produce an outcome, other times someone else makes the choice that affects our outcome.

The other part of the question asks about the future and working on other projects. I think this is potentially the start of other projects, yes. In fact, completing this book and realizing that there are hundreds of other things we could talk about and that questions may arise from readers means there are sequels on the horizon, I can see them now!

What are you hoping to achieve with this book? What have learnt from writing this book?
Ciarán answers: I'm hoping that people actually learn about both sides, that they take something away from your perspective and something from mine. If, after reading what I've got to say, they still come away interpreting their personal experience as paranormal then there is nothing I can say otherwise. I'm also hoping that it encourages people to listen to every side of an argument before making an informed decision.

I've learnt a lot. I've also learnt a lot about my views on things I've never previously been asked about. I've found further evidence in your words and answers for the idea that cynicism and dogmatism are not two separate classifications but exist at two opposite, and extreme, ends of a long continuum, a long line of scepticism and belief. I've learnt that you can't necessarily place a person at one end of that line, or even position them at some point along it. It wholly depends on what you're asking them about. In this book we've asked each other many questions, covered many topics and our answers have varied. Sometimes they've been expected and sometimes a surprise.

The Parapsychologist questions the Clairvoyant
- Ciarán asks Billy

Have you ever provided any information to the police in a criminal investigation? I should say 'psychic' or 'mediumship' information. That is, have you ever earned the title 'psychic detective'? If yes, why did you feel the need? If not, why?

Billy answers: The only time I dared offer information to the police was during the murder investigation of school girl Milly Towler (I think that was her name.) I did this on the advice of a journalist friend who gave me a special Scotland Yard number to ring. I was interviewed for forty minutes about the nature of my information, which had all come through reoccurring dreams. Although the content of the dreams was quite clear and consistent; the name of a lane, description of the perpetrator, and other explicit details, I never heard from the police again. However, they did give me a code to keep for my own information, just in case it went further.

It's interesting that you say that there are particular astrological signs that make good mediums and then you list mediumistic attributes for all of the signs. Please comment.

Billy answers: This concept came about as a result of 25 years of making a detailed analysis of the various signs. All astrological signs do have their particular psychic characteristics. Some individuals thrive on being in the public eye and others do not. There is a negative and a positive side to each sign. Some signs are naturally communicators; some are thoughtful and compassionate and shy clear of the public eye. My theory has no scientific bearing, but I know that it works, and I use it when training mediums in my centre. The more sensitive the sign, the more susceptible it is to outside influences.

If mediums potentially leave themselves 'wide open to ridicule' by taking part in scientific experiments, why did you?
Billy answers: This is a fare comment. I only did this for you. I felt comfortable that you would not set me up. I may have been wrong in my assumption, but I did it for a friend, nothing more. In saying that, I would not do it again.

I find the concept of Spirit Guides absolutely fascinating. Why do Spirit Guides invariably tend to be foreign (e.g. Native American, French etc)? Given that the majority of mediums I have dealt with have foreign Spirit Guides why are none of the mediums able to converse in the language of their guide?
Billy answers: First of all, I think it's a general consensus of opinion that the barrier of language is somehow lifted when communication takes place between the medium and the Spirit Guide. I can only really speak for myself, having had a very close relationship with Tall Pine since I was a baby. Although T.P - as he is affectionately known - appears as a Native American, I always believed from the Sioux nation, over the last decade or so I have discovered that Tall Pine is a sort of conglomeration of personalities, and the figure head of a group known to me as 'The Elders'. As far back as I can recall Tall Pine had been an integral part of my life. Whenever I saw Tall Pine as a child he was as solid and tangible as any other person, and never appeared to me as some vague and extremely nebulous phantom as depicted in 'Spooky' films and other such ideas created by the writer's imagination. Tall Pine was very real. I could hear him quite clearly, even though the dialogue that transpired between us was purely telepathic, without one word being spoken. Right up until my mid-teens I could never see the point of Tall Pine. Apart from the fact that he had always been there, he never really seemed to do anything other than make me aware of his presence.

I personally believe that Spirit Guides are facets of our own personalities; as we develop spiritually, so they change. It is the Spiritualist belief that Native Americans were in fact closer to the earth. I knew one veteran medium whose Spirit Guide was a Cockney Refuge Collector. In my early years as a professional medium, I used to receive regular communication from a German speaking gentleman who simply refused to use any other mode of communication except speech. The last thing he said to me before he disappeared into oblivion was: 'Sprechen ist Silbern, Schweigen ist Goldern'. (Speech is Silver, Silence is Golden.) That meant something to me at that particular time.

Having been mediumistically inclined since I was a child, I have grown up with the notion that I was being guided by certain discarnate beings, one of whom I had always known as 'Tall Pine', a Native American. So, what are Spirit Guides all about?

According to Spiritualist philosophy so-called Spirit Guides are discarnate entities, long since passed from this world, who attach themselves to selected individuals to give them spiritual guidance. More than this though, Spirit Guides are, more often than not, integral parts of a soul group, whose sole intention is to help the evolution of the individual soul. In fact, it was only in the last few years or so that I learned that Tall Pine was in fact a conglomeration of souls, the combination of which make up a group I now know as the 'Elders', wise discarnate individuals who have always helped me with the various aspects of my work. I do have a theory that our Spirit Guides are no more than facets of our own personality, and that we more or less create them in the subliminal areas of our minds, just as one would create a thought form. Once this image has been created, we then endow it with a certain degree of intelligence and thus give it life. I'm not suggesting that this is the case with all so-called Spirit Guides, but over the years I have become more than a little sceptical about the whole subject. However, it's a very comforting thought that we are being looked after by superior spiritual beings, ambassadors of an even greater, omnipotent, omnipresent being. In fact, the majority of people find the concept of Spirit Guides quite fascinating and even the most sceptical of people secretly want to believe that someone or even something is watching over them in times of great need.

I love the topic of ethics, ethics in giving readings or visiting an allegedly haunted house. You mention that many mediums operate ethically, including yourself, yet having the intention and awareness is not enough. Mediums constantly deal with vulnerable people all the time. I feel if there is no understanding of bereavement counselling then leave well alone. Also mediums frequently, especially in haunting investigations, operate outside of their 'area of expertise' and handle EMF meters or laser thermometers without understanding why. Care to comment, perhaps suggest reasons why this happens, and perhaps any suggestions for the future?

Billy answers: I have always believed that when a recently bereaved person consults me that it is wrong to even attempt any form of communication, and that it is far more beneficial to the person just to talk - perhaps even to explain the nature of death and the process of life on the 'other side'. I must say that I very rarely charge a fee for this, nor do I charge anyone who is obviously distressed during the reading. I, like most mediums, work to a code of ethics; I do know how far I should go when entering the emotional mine field with someone who is, as you described, vulnerable. A lot of mediums do tread clumsily in; however, I prefer to leave well alone. Regarding the use of EMF meters etc: Although I do possess such gadgets I don't use them. I only have them as visual aids in lectures and workshops. If I'm honest, a lot of inexperienced mediums use their undeveloped skills without any understanding of how they work and why. In my opinion, mediums should learn what exactly is going on in their own psyche before they venture into the dark. God knows what's out there. This is why I do feel that presenters on paranormal television programmes such as *Most Haunted* should take great care. There are hidden and extremely dangerous surprises deep within the subconscious areas of the mind that can have all sorts of repercussions later on. The inexperienced are playing on a psychological and metaphysical mine field. Both good and bad spirits know how to play games, and they play to their own rules.

You seem to be quite down on psychics and mediums, am I wrong? If it is the case, what can mediums, and psychics, of today really offer us?

Billy answers: I know it would seem to many that I have become the Judas medium, but in all fairness I have become very disillusioned with most of the mediumistic profession. Today it is very difficult to know who is genuine and who is not. I think the general public should be aware of the bogus clairvoyants and mediums offering their services today. If you had have asked me this question 25 years ago I would have said mediums do extremely worthwhile work, and can, at their best, take away the fear of death. All that it has done for me is make me fear my own mortality, and looking at the so-called television mediums, I do wonder what on earth it is all about. Sour Grapes? Not at all! I have appeared on television all over the world, and been involved in some superb investigations. But when you have worked with the best, and become good friends with the rest, you begin to see exactly how they work, and believe me it's quite frightening. This is why I am now working in completely different areas.

What would convince you of my sceptical argument? What would convince you that there is nothing out there?!

Billy answers: I have to be very careful at this point, because I have a feeling that I have led you into the centre of the ice-covered lake. I know there is something out there, but I do believe it is nothing whatsoever like mediums believe. I believe in the Devachanic states of Hinduism and Buddhism. These are the realms of the gods; the formless worlds of pure experiences. I refer you to a previous statement: Mediumship requires a little more than faith and belief.

What have you learnt from writing this book?

Billy answers: The whole process has been a psychological as well as a spiritual exercise. It's made me analyse more closely my own beliefs, and certainly helped me to have a different perspective of the whole spectrum of the paranormal.

Final Thoughts

The Clairvoyant - Billy Roberts
The Good Old Days

I do wonder if the mediums of bygone days were really as good as we are led to believe they were, or if their reputations have been somewhat distorted and blow up out of all proportion through the passage of time? Were the veteran mediums of Spiritualism any different to the mediums of Spiritualism today? Has anything really changed about mediums other than the fact that today they can demonstrate their skills in theatres and hotel function rooms? I used to listen intently to my Aunt Louise's stories (and she was a veteran medium) about this medium or that medium and about the various phenomena she experienced whilst sitting in circles all over the UK. But, to be quite honest, looking back they were really just stories, and like all incredible stories, unless we witness them for ourselves, then that's all they are, just stories. How many times have you been told about the excellent and evidential messages given by a particular medium, and yet when you see the medium demonstrating for yourself you are left feeling somewhat confused and disappointed, simply because they are nothing whatsoever like you were told? There is little wonder that psychologists, parapsychologists and sceptics pour so much disdain and cynicism on the whole concept of mediumship when, as I have previously said, it really cannot stand up to close scientific or psychological scrutiny, regardless of what anyone thinks. I know this statement will bring a great deal of criticism from some people, and may even prompt others to write to me in defence of their favourite mediums, but I have to refer you to my previous statement, it's still just a story or, at least, your opinion - just as this, of course, is my opinion.

As far as I am concerned mediumistic skills require a little more than faith and belief in a Spirit World, and because a medium is well known or appears on television does not necessarily mean he or she is sincere or even genuine - far from it! The majority of the mediums I have known have begun their mediumistic work primarily because another medium has told him or her that this is the path that they should follow. The other minority have been led into their mediumistic work, either because they were brought up in a Spiritualist family, or because of some experience he or she has had, traumatic or otherwise. However, the majority of mediums do nearly always affirm that they have been mediumistic since they were young, regardless of whether or not this is true. To be fair, the majority of people have had some sort of paranormal experience at some time in their life, and whether that constitutes a natural tendency towards mediumship or not, is in fact a matter of opinion. Almost anyone can claim to be mediumistic, and proving otherwise would, in most cases, be quite difficult. This is the only problem I personally have with the mediumistic profession in general; and until the laws change with mediums and the paranormal as a whole, then I am afraid we are left to the mercy of those unscrupulous charlatans who prey upon the vulnerable and the stupid people who make a habit of visiting mediums for no other reason than to find out what the future holds. Although somewhat of a cliché, I will go as far as to say that 'mediums are rare'. They are most certainly not found on every street corner, every shop window or in every newspaper. Psychics may be found everywhere, but mediums are born and most certainly not made!

The Parapsychologist - Ciarán O'Keeffe

"We soon learn that there is nothing mysterious or supernatural in the case, but that all proceeds from the usual propensity of mankind towards the marvellous, and that, though this inclination may at intervals receive a check from sense and learning, it can never be thoroughly extirpated from human nature."
- David Hume, [Eighteenth-century Scottish philosopher, economist & historian.]

The world of the paranormal is a wondrous place. Practitioners, like Billy, have a unique personal insight into this place and provide an alternative paranormal point of view that may seem more magical, more wondrous than mine. I too have a sense of wonderment at the discoveries I regularly make when reading various books or talking to people about their experiences. The scientific journey, for me, is comparable to any magical one. If such a journey is, in addition, looking at the science of the paranormal then it surely is as magical. The psychologist Vyse said "…it is not necessary to give the sunset supernatural meaning to be humbled by its magnificence." In the same way I am humbled by the complexities of human experience and behaviour. Humbled by the complexity of parts I don't understand and humbled by the simplicity of those I now do.

Further Reading

The following is a list of books and websites that Billy and Ciarán have either mentioned in the book or are recommending for those interested in reading more about the topic.

The Clairvoyant - Billy Roberts:
Website: www.billyroberts.co.uk
* *MASTER YOUR PSYCHIC POWERS* by Billy Roberts (Published by Cassell.)
* *BILLY ROBERTS' TEN STEP PSYCHIC DEVELOPMENT PROGRAMME* by Billy Roberts (Published by Piatkus.)
* *THE MAGIC OF THE AURA* by Billy Roberts (Published by Apex Publishing Ltd)
* *THE FIRST PRINCIPLES OF THEOSOPHY* by JINARAJADASA (Published by the Theosophical society.)
* *PSYCHIC DISCOVERIES* by Sheila Ostrander & Lynn Schroeder (Published by Souvenir Press.)
* *FOURTEEN LESSONS IN YOGI PHILOSOPHY AND ORIENTAL OCCULTISM* by YOGI RAMACHARAKA (Published by LN FOWLER.)
* *SCIENCE OF BREATH* by YOGI RAMACHARAKA (Published by LN FOWLER.)
* *THE UNEXPLAINED - PSYCHIC POWERS* by Simon Tomlin (Published by PARRAGON.)

The Parapsychologist - Ciarán O'Keeffe:
Website: www.theparapsychologist.com
* Broughton, R. (1992). *Parapsychology: The controversial science.* London: Random Century Group.
* Carroll, R.T. (2003). *The Skeptic's Dictionary.* New Jersey: John Wiley & Sons. (See also: www.skepdic.com)
* Edge, H. L., Morris, R. L., Palmer, J. & Rush, J. H. (eds). (1987). *Foundations of Parapsychology: Exploring the boundaries of human*

capability. London: Routledge & Kegan Paul Ltd.
* Fielding, Y. & O'Keeffe, C. (2006). *Ghost Hunters: A guide to investigating the paranormal*. London: Hodder & Stoughton.
* Gauld, A. (1982). *Mediumship and survival*. London: William Heinemann Ltd.
* Hayes, N. (2000). *Foundations of Psychology*. London: Thomson Learning.
* Hyman, R. (1989). *The Elusive Quarry*. New York: Prometheus Books.
* Lyons, A. & Truzzi, M. (1991). *The Blue Sense: Psychic detectives and crime*. New York: Warner Books.
* Marks, D., & Kammann, R. (1980). *The Psychology of the Psychic*. New York: Prometheus Books.
* Melton, G. J. (ed). (2001). *Encyclopedia of Occultism & Parapsychology*. Farmington Hills, MI: Gale Group, Inc.
* O'Keeffe, C. & Wiseman, R. (2005). Testing alleged mediumship. *British Journal of Psychology*, 96, pp215-231.
* Rowland, I. (2002). *The Full Facts Book of Cold Reading*. London: Ian Roland Limited.
* Tannen, D. (1996). *Talking Voices: Repetition, dialogue and imagery in conversational discourse*. Cambridge: Cambridge University Press.

Every effort to include brief quotes from various psychics and mediums has been done in strict accordance with the 'fair use' practice as detailed in the relevant books. All such quotes have been introduced merely for illustrative purposes and no opinion on their veracity or genuineness has been presented. Readers are encouraged to consult the writings of any psychics and mediums mentioned by Billy or Ciarán in order to read the passages in which they were originally quoted to see that they were not taken out of context.